# RICHARD KEATING

Selected and Current Works

THE MASTER ARCHITECT SERIES II

# RICHARD KEATING

Selected and Current Works

First published in Australia in 1996 by
The Images Publishing Group Pty Ltd
ACN 059 734 431
6 Bastow Place, Mulgrave, Victoria, 3170
Telephone (61 3) 9561 5544 Facsimile (61 3) 9561 4860

National Library of Australia Cataloguing-in-Publication Data

    Keating, Richard
       Richard Keating: selected and current works.

       Bibliography.
       Includes index.
       ISBN 1 875498 51 6
       Master Architect Series ISSN 1320 7253

       1. Keating, Richard. 2. Architecture, American.
       3. Architecture, Modern—20thCentury—United States
       I. Title. (Series: Master architect series. 2).

  720.92

Edited by Stephen Dobney
Designed by The Graphic Image Studio Pty Ltd,
Mulgrave, Australia
Film separation by Scanagraphix Pty Ltd Australia
Printing by Everbest Printing H.K.

# Contents

# Introduction

# Introduction

## Richard Keating—An Essay

By Kay Kaiser

"Light-footed elegance"—the phrase was used by a German publication to describe Richard Keating's winning entry for the Opel Kreisel Building, a 26-story office building proposed as a visual gateway on a prominent but difficult site northwest of Frankfurt's city center. It's doubtful that the headline writer realized how aptly the phrase described the most consistent quality in Keating's body of work, and the architect himself.

An elegance of form and detail defines the towers built by Skidmore, Owings & Merrill in Texas and California in the late 70s and 80s while Keating was head of their Houston and Los Angeles offices. It's obvious that from the beginning of his career, Keating and those close to him were intent on finding methods to create well-made buildings using the technology of the day. Several of the projects are monolithic corporate expressions while others are precise, spare and light. Structure is expressed and often exposed. Layered or eroded walls mitigate the mass of the towers and often appear to float above the ground plane. Fine detail and transparency at the bases allow the enormous towers to fit graciously into the streetscape. Keating and his associates have found methods of containing millions of square feet in a box that doesn't seem unduly overwrought. In most cases, observers forget that the building's chassis is a box because they are so taken with the sculptural dynamics of the top, bottom and edges.

This is the work of a new breed of modernists who also recognize the requirements of the contemporary marketplace. Leasing agents appreciate the plans in their own way. Despite the movement in the form on the exterior, the interior spaces are regular and flexible, the core areas are contained and efficient, and vertical and lateral circulation systems are where one would expect to find them. Many would consider this synthesis of aesthetics and function as extremely light-footed architectural manipulation. To others it seems like slight-of-hand.

Richard Keating as a person is equally nimble. He's quick in movement and speech, he's intense, socially adroit and a forceful boardroom negotiator. Other architects are intimidated by his personal elegance and his client list, which includes Trammell Crow, Hines Interests, Hewlett Packard, Equitable, British Petroleum, BMC Software, Houston Industries, Prudential, and the State of California. He is seen as a prodigy whose rapid ascension through the ranks of Skidmore, Owings & Merrill, America's corporate architecture giant, is legendary. He joined SOM's Chicago office at 24 after graduating from the University of California at Berkeley. In 1976, at the age of 32, he was asked to open an office for SOM in Houston, Texas. Eventually he found himself in charge of 200 architects, interior designers and engineers. Press releases say that during Keating's 10-year stewardship, the office completed nearly 40 million square feet of work, most of it rising extremely vertically from the plains.

In 1986, after the Texas boom was officially over, he went to Los Angeles to reinvigorate SOM's office there. He was 42 at the time. Four years later he resigned from SOM to open his own office, Keating Mann Jernigan Rottet, in Los Angeles, taking with him Michael Mann, Robert Jernigan, Lauren Rottet, Paul Danna, Jose Palacios and many others from the Texas/California team.

At the end of 1994 the 60-person firm merged with Daniel, Mann, Johnson & Mendenhall (DMJM), another giant with a long history in Los Angeles. Keating had turned 50 six months earlier.

Keating explains the reason for the merger: "The world had changed. Even with 60 people at KMJR it was difficult to compete for large-scale work in the essentially disappearing high-rise and high-end interiors arena. To work in Latin and South America, and Southeast Asia, you need considerable resources to travel, to staff remote projects, and frankly at KMJR that depth wasn't possible. We either had to get smaller and be a design consultant to larger offices, or be part of a larger organization. DMJM is so strong in terms of transportation planning, engineering and program management.

"There is no other firm in California that is as stable; however, it has been more focused on vast engineering and institutional projects rather than architecture which, relatively speaking, comprised a much smaller work base. It seemed that it was a great opportunity to marry all these former SOM people to this extremely solid engineering firm. As design director of DMJM overall, I can be involved in any project. This would increase the spread and variety of my project types and make more public sector work possible—not since the 20s and 30s have we seen so much attention to well-designed public sector projects all over the country."

He sounds like an architect on top of the world when he speaks of an organization that "sits in Southern California and can go anywhere it wants."

This is architecture in the fast lane. Thinking about leading an enormous office through projects on this scale is so foreign to many architects that they regard Keating's world as something other than architecture. It's business. It's management. It's promotion. But is it design in the traditional sense in which a personal vision rises off the paper to become a building, a part of a city? The question makes many people uneasy around Keating. They don't know exactly what kind of architect he is.

There are many sides to Keating. Sometimes the statements he makes, depending on the circumstances and the company, add to the confusion. He can sound extremely calculating: "If you're going to play, you go with the flow and play with those who have the power. The attraction to SOM was that it seemed to open up access to larger-than-life ambitions. It's an ego trip to make a tall building, but it's more than that. It's a rare mathematical game that certain people can play."

But there is another side: "If you think about everything nature creates, most of it is horizontal because of gravity. The lifting up of the mountain is the holy part. From Stonehenge to the Sears Tower, man wanted to do something to mark the place. But in that marking, some plan of humanity must be inherent. The lifting up of the rock has to mean something to more than one person. The tower represents the soaring part of our self-understanding. It represents more to one's soul than a Quonset hut. And the art of the tower is something more than accommodating the function or accomplishing the engineering."

At times he has compared his function to that of an orchestra conductor. "Architecture, like music, is about moments. There are times when the soloist is performing, but at other times the entire ensemble has to work as one. It's the conductor's job to make both situations happen at the right point."

He has also said that the individual practitioner, someone he characterizes as a man in a cape who makes all the decisions, is limited to small projects. "For large-scale work, we need a team of structural and mechanical engineers, architects, interior designers and many others. The lead architect must have his ego under control and not be sensitive about where the ideas come from. Any other way, and the good people won't work for you for very long."

It's a testament to the collaborative ideal that this group has been together nearly 20 years, which brings a consistency to the design effort. Although he wonders about the structure of the SOM corporate framework in recent decades, he continues to use the original vision of Nathaniel Owings as a guide. "Owings was trying to create a system of people who could play in the big league to redefine urban America," he says. "That vision sustained the firm. At SOM and afterward, I gathered as colleagues and partners the best people I knew. Their sophistication and technical ability are extraordinary. And I've come to realize that I enjoy empowering others to act on what they know."

In saying that, it sounds as though he was born to corporate architecture. But just when you start believing that, Keating throws in a curve. He explains that no one is more surprised by the turns his career has taken than he is. When he went to Skidmore's Chicago office, he planned to stay only a few years. His objective was to gain first-hand experience in tall building design and construction and then return to Berkeley to spend the rest of his life as an architectural historian, teaching and writing about modernism, urbanism and tall building technology. The plan changed when it became apparent how unusually agile and able he was at putting large projects together. He was skilled in talking to developers and city officials.

Eight years later he found himself in charge of the Houston office. "When hiring people, I had to tell them something that explained what we were about. I invented my own purist version that had to do with collaboration—engineering in connection with architecture and being a designer at the same time. I had no design mentors close at hand in Houston. Chuck Bassett was in San Francisco, a long way away. I was shot into the void and had to feel my way through. I was helped by the early experience I received from Walter Netsch, the man who brought me into the firm, and by just living in Chicago. And I like to say that Bruce Graham taught me everything I know about how to look at architecture. Bruce gave me the opportunity to either hang myself or succeed. He also taught me about power. Bruce's energy, his ability to charge through walls, and similar energy in others such as Bill Hartman, represented the essence of Skidmore, Owings & Merrill."

But in the late 70s, Keating says, architects from Steven Holl to Michael Graves were designing very small, thoughtful projects. "And there I was with one enormous project after another. First, I was in a different world. It was a growing period. The biggest influence on Texas style at the time was Philip Johnson, who had the ear of all the clients we were pursuing. We had to work our way through that period of romantic imagery, but we survived that, too. Now I'm relieved that the bones of the buildings are carrying the message.

"But in my world of Texas architecture, it was difficult to divorce the path I was seeing in design from the overwhelming involvement of the problem-solving aspects of real estate. The basic purpose of an office building is clearly defined function. It's a box. It allows people to move in and out. There can't be anything about the architecture that's compromising. From floor three to a few floors below the top, the building must be pretty basic, reduced to its essence. This is the part of the building that makes money. The core elements must be organized so they don't intrude on the lease spaces. But you have to be able to shift gears. Floor one through three are about how the building inserts itself into the pedestrian pattern of the city. If you place the intensity there, everybody appropriately comprehends the building. That's where you concentrate on the grain of materials, the fine detail in handrails and landscape. At the top, the building can be expressive. A high-rise can't be all one idea from top to bottom.

"The design process is loaded with objective and subjective decisions. Which way to orient the building, what should the spans be, the dimensions of core to window walls. Those are the objective decisions, along with budget. You might want the exterior to be platinum, but if you've only got the money for chain link, you better find out what you can do with chain link. Economics is always the most real part of the program."

He learned another aspect of architectural economics early on in Houston. Mega-developer Gerald Hines was the force everyone believed would sustain the SOM office in its early years, but just as Keating arrived, Hines took his business elsewhere. "It was a fight for survival until I found Trammell Crow. For me, Houston happened too hard, too fast. I had to unlearn a lot through the later years. There's survival, sure, but there must be humanity in there somewhere, too."

Looking back, Keating laughingly describes the Texas experience as the decade he was "buffeted by winds of the bizarre." Part of the battering was caused by the speed and enormity of growth in the Sunbelt states in the 70s. He remembers a client who owned 25,000 apartment units free and clear. Keating imagined the man's house filling up to the rafters with rent checks every month. "He had so much money he didn't know what to do with it, so he came to our office one day and said he wanted a 45-story high-rise like the ones he saw us building for everyone else. We built one for him. He also wanted a $5 million restaurant where he could sing to his friends. We didn't do that one. There were people worth hundreds of millions of dollars, but 20 years before, they were starting out on career paths that didn't promise that kind of financial success.

"The roots of Dallas were in the mercantile trade. The goods came from other places, mainly New York. Developers in Dallas looked to European architectural models that expressed the solidity of old wealth. Houston was a different story. There they said it was all right that they made their fortunes 20 seconds ago, and many of them did, as wildcatters in the oil fields. It was a blue-collar city, a technology-based place defined by pipelines and shipping. Developers there were far more receptive to modern, technological expressions. As architects, we attempted to express the culture of these two very different cities. There's no doubt that we were the beneficiaries of growth in the Sunbelt, but it was a difficult place to develop a practice of architecture as an art since everything moved so quickly and with such specific focus on economics."

And yet it was during this period that he and his team made the effort to find a design signature for their work. The identifying elements were highly refined details and use of materials. Even when the budget was $55 a square foot, it was obvious that the team had been manipulating materials for high effect. From Houston to Los Angeles, Keating has encouraged everyone in the office to search for material sources that were beyond what was usually found in most architects' sample rooms. So great was his enthusiasm, that the gathering process took on a life of its own.

He says he likes to sit in the materials room, a place he regards as his sandbox of sorts, and enjoy all the possibilities that it contains. Every stone, every finish, every texture. Every type of glass with various coating densities. All cut in one foot square pieces and organized thoughtfully. For him, the process of selection is pure play. Finding something new that pushes technology forward or something that could be used in a new way is pure joy. He was delighted when he found a stainless steel jet fuel filter and subsequently the material was used as a wall surface in the First Interstate Bank in Los Angeles. Later he wanted to use a larger-scale version of woven stainless steel as a walking surface in a lawyer's office. Hot rolled steel was cut into two-foot squares and became a floor surface in his own office. He's fascinated with a ceramic material from Japan that looks like milky glass, but when its backlit, it ranges in color from powder blue to orange. The material was used in the BMC building in Houston. New York glass artist James Carpenter brought his methods of working with layered and dichroic glass to several projects. Although never implemented, Carpenter developed for the Gas Company Tower in Los Angeles a glass rod truss wall on the lower three stories of curtain wall. The glass rods would have served as the major compression elements of the system as they appeared to float in space and created a grid of luminous color. Carpenter and Keating often try to collaborate on a wide variety of projects.

In the Texas days, the architects found a company in California that had a large autoclave used for making acrylic panels for deep-sea research vessels and aquarium walls. The four-inch thick, five foot square panels found their way into the spire at the top of the Trammell Crow Center in Dallas, and into Keating's own furniture.

The cowhide linings of the elevator cabs at BMC are a particular delight for Keating. He made a jig of the panel dimensions and laid it over the hides to get the white spots exactly where he wanted them. Years later, he still remembers that there are 32 panels per cab. The fact that the hides came from Northern Italian cows and now line elevators in Texas is another source of humor for him.

Joining materials together tightly, crisply, and with attention to proportion, texture and color is another mutual passion among the architects in this group. Keating names Mies van der Rohe, Gordon Bunshaft and Fumihiko Maki as architects who have achieved the degree of refinement he's searching for. As is the habit of many architects whose ability to criticize themselves is fully developed, he identifies only sections of buildings that he feels worked out well in terms of materials and precision.

In the BMC lobby, the confluence of the copper wall that was horizontally laced with half-inch stainless steel bar stock and the aluminum-clad core elements meets Keating's criteria. One plane is clearly delineated from another through changes in materials. He is proud of the view as one looks up through the rotunda of the Gas Company Tower in Los Angeles to the lobby. Here, the core is clad in limestone and the other interior wall elements are aluminum panels with exposed stainless steel fasteners. At ICM Headquarters in Beverly Hills, he's pleased with the limestone, wood, and stainless steel elevator lobby and cabs. The lobby walls are a combination of buff and striated Indiana limestone and glass. The call lanterns are incorporated into the glass walls of the elevator lobby.

The shift to Los Angeles was responsible for Keating working at a different scale. He, and the nucleus of people he brought with him, had to slow down and evaluate what it meant to build in Los Angeles. The first projects were small. Connections to the street became more fully developed because, unlike Dallas and Houston, most sections of LA had an established street life. Designing for an impact on the skyline was no longer a key consideration either for the architects or their clients.

He considers the 1988 commission to design the Gas Company Tower as a turning point in his career. "Finally, my own sensitivities as an architect and those of the client crossed perfectly," he said.

He describes Robert Maguire as a client who had a vision for the city that was larger than a dream of an individual monument to himself. Now that it's built, the tower is admired for the graceful moves in glass and metal on its shaft and crown, but it's also being used as a model for the creative collaboration between public and private sector interests. Maguire, who has long been an advocate of downtown Los Angeles, devised a favorable exchange with the City to allow for the maximum development of the site while physically and economically contributing to the rebuilding of the Central Library and Pershing Square.

Keating's ground plan and entrances were designed to connect with the public square and library building. A network of shops, landscaping, and art connects the new building to the streetscape.

"The problem was how to suture pedestrian systems into the building. The antithesis is to just drop the building down. But there's more to it than just adding retail at the bottom. It's being thoughtful about how people move through a city—from public to semi-public, to semi-private to private ... Landscaping is the one thread in a city. It should never be used just to blur the edge of a building."

It may be significant that his interest in landscape has increased since coming to Los Angeles. The change may have little to do with working in a climate that's more hospitable to plants than Texas, since a large amount of the recent work remains in Texas. More likely, the cause is an understanding that cities don't need more big buildings that are designed as objects without regard for the surroundings. In the announcement of the DMJM–Keating merger, he expressed the idea this way: "The future of architecture leads conclusively toward both international activity and a broadening of services focused on the wisdom of solutions rather than on imagery and form. The needs of today in the US have shifted and focus more on the larger urban issues rather than private investment and individual statements of high-rise office towers."

In Bangkok, Thailand, the team is working on a 12 million square foot office, retail, and hotel complex that must also serve as a bus terminal that can accommodate 800 bus arrivals and departures every hour. For a complex in Monterrey, Mexico, the problem was to discover spatial methods of creating a sense of place. Projects in Korea and Jakarta present other urban planning issues to be resolved. "That gives you, as an architect, a different level of responsibility. All too often there's a big chase to make a dollar and then we see the exportation of tired images without real concern for urbanity. It's the exportation of architecture, but not planning."

Many times in conversation, Keating comes back to Nathaniel Owings, the SOM founder who fascinated him more than the others. First, he always says he admired Owings for the collaborative process he brought to the firm. He became Keating's symbol of organization, energy, and direction. But after a while, he voices the real reason for the admiration: "He wasn't a sociologist or a historian. He was an architect who was looking for ways architecture could affect entire places."

Keating remembers in particular Owings' victory in which he stopped a horrendous plan to build an elevated freeway bridge through Baltimore's Inner Harbor in the late 60s. "His planning effort, coupled with the right vision and access to power not only stopped the plan but offered an alternative that got built and changed the entire city," Keating said. Others who were around at the time said that Owings wasn't afraid of anyone. He took on the governor of Maryland and his pro-bridge henchmen and won.

It doesn't take an enormous intuitive leap to imagine Keating evolving into a similar role. After the mastery of urban form and urban process, perhaps it's the next logical step to serve as a guardian of cities. Good architects armed with conscience and acute perceptions have taken that step before. Maybe Keating will be the next.

So much of what constitutes office work and its architectural accommodation is generic. The physical object of the office building becomes somewhat of a formulaic planning system with unique characteristics in the public spaces and how the building, as a whole, is made as well as how it takes its position among others urbanistically, and/or creates a publicly perceived sense of place.

This work does not shy from the formula of the plan, but seeks to optimize it as an accommodation of the function. It recognizes that the speculative office building is essentially financial machinery to maximize return from tenants to investment in construction while ultimately creating lasting and potentially increased overall value.

The office building has been the building block of our cities for most of the 20th century and as such is most often engaged in an additive role to the public perception and comprehension of urban place. This means that its positioning, public spaces, circulation sequences, and often material choices should be considered as part of a larger entity. This work has that understanding at its core. Each building has been derived from its setting and seen as a considerate addition to the urban fabric.

Ultra-high-rise buildings of seventy stories or more have yet another layer of technological concerns that the optimization process yields as potential for the architectural expression. The lateral loading conditions of wind and sometimes seismic activity as well as vertical transportation, and life safety requirements make these buildings substantially unique. In addition their very height and scale create a special perspective as an urban object. This work seeks to define itself around these parameters utilizing special structural systems, aerolastic dampening, spoilers, and wind apertures while simultaneously accommodating the most efficient means of transporting people and materials and planning for their safety as well.

## Corporate Architecture

# First Federal Savings and Loan

Design/Completion 1978/1980
Little Rock, Arkansas
First Federal Savings
158,000 square feet
Skidmore, Owings & Merrill,
Richard Keating, Design Partner
Steel frame
Caledonia granite, glass, aluminum

First Federal Savings Plaza features a
light-filled atrium flanked by seven floors
of executive office space. The atrium
roofline steps down in one-story
increments from the building's full height
to the fourth level. The 90 x 90 foot space
serves as the banking hall and is bordered
by a garden of seasonal flowers. The white
interior walls and clear insulated glass set
the lobby off from the bronze aluminum
and bronze reflective glass of the exterior.
Floors and tables of polished St Laurent
marble combine with the warm colors
of the carpeting and furnishings and are
highlighted by polished stainless steel
details throughout.

1

1　Interior view, interconnecting stair
2　Atrium banking hall

2

## Allied Bank Plaza

Design/Completion 1979/1983
Houston, Texas
Century Development Corporation
Skidmore, Owings & Merrill,
Edward Charles Bassett, Partner in Charge
Richard Keating, Design Partner
1,800,000 square feet
Trussed steel tube
Green reflective glass and stainless steel curtain wall,
black granite base

The 71-story Allied Bank Tower (now First Interstate Plaza) is located essentially at the center of downtown Houston. The tower is sited so that its flat sides are in alignment with neighboring facades, unifying the buildings and the skyline. The semi-curved form was achieved by juxtaposing two quarter-cylinder shafts which are offset by one bay. The combination of planes and curves allows for the constant interplay of sunlight on the tower's surface and also reduces the building's substantial mass.

In contrast to the surrounding dark granite high-rises, this building is light and fluid, with its upper 70 stories clad in an uninterrupted skin of reflective green glass. At grade, the building is sheathed in polished black granite with a 5-foot stainless steel band capping the junction of the granite and glass. This use of rich materials and careful detailing also provides a human-scaled sense of entry to the building.

*Continued*

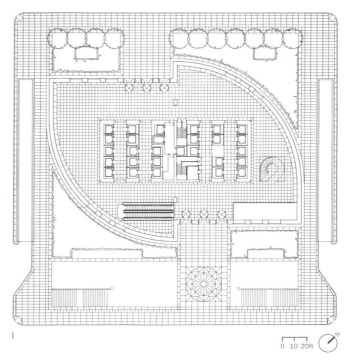

1

0 10 20ft

2

1   Site plan
2   Houston skyline
3   North view

22

3

Approximately 65 per cent of users enter the building through Houston's downtown pedestrian tunnel system which protects against the city's infamous heat, rain, and humidity. As the tunnel enters the building it becomes a glass corridor, bisecting a sunken plaza which provides views and sunlight to the underground path. Double-deck express elevators shuttle passengers to skylobbies on floors 34–35 and 58–59, where they transfer to local elevators. This arrangement keeps the core to a manageable size—there are 27 elevator shafts running 56 cabs.

The lower skylobby incorporates horizontal trusses tying together the bundled tube structural systems in each half of the plan. These structural elements are prominent in the two-floor public space and are clad in white paneled wood casings rather than in a high-tech material.

4

# Bank of the Southwest Tower Competition

Design 1983
Houston, Texas
Century Development Corporation
Skidmore, Owings & Merrill,
Richard Keating, Design Partner
2,300,000 square feet
Trussed steel tube
Granite, travertine, glass

The proposed design for the Bank of the Southwest Tower accommodates a varied program of office and retail. As designed, the weight of the building is carried at its corners, allowing the structural elements to be extended above the roofline of the tower to support a second building which is circular in form and topped by glass. The restaurant occupies several tiers of space under the glass dome and the observation levels are located immediately below. In what would have been the second tallest building in the world, at 1,370 feet, a 360 degree view of the Texas countryside would have been possible.

At the ground level, an expansive plaza results from the structural concepts, as well as a daylight park at the tunnel level. The four structural pedestals at the corners house lobbies, three of which carry the identities of major tenants at the street and tunnel levels. The fourth pedestal contains the service elevators as well as the lobby for the observation and restaurant levels.

1

1   South view
2   Southeast view

## San Felipe Plaza

Design/Completion 1982/1984
Houston, Texas
The Farb Companies
Skidmore, Owings & Merrill,
Richard Keating, Design Partner
1,000,000 square feet
Slip formed concrete core, steel frame
Polished Caledonia gray-brown granite,
glass, stainless steel

San Felipe Plaza is a 45-story office tower
located outside the central business
district of Houston. In response to its
somewhat suburban setting and resulting
high visibility, the tower was sculpturally
formed to have an ever-changing presence
depending on vantage point and light
conditions. The curved facade elongates
the perspective view of the tower, giving it
a thin, elegant appearance. This is
enhanced by a cascade of setbacks and
glass, circularly detailed as a counterpoint
to the main frame of granite and glass.

1

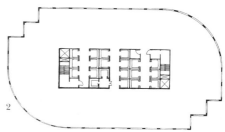

2

1   East view
2   Site plan
3   Entry court

3

4

5

6

# Trammell Crow Center

Design/Completion 1981/1985
Dallas, Texas
Trammell Crow Company
Skidmore, Owings & Merrill,
Richard Keating, Design Partner
1,750,000 square feet
Steel frame
Polished and flame-cut autumn brown granite, bronze
reflective glass

The first of three high-rise buildings
designed by Keating in downtown Dallas,
the Trammell Crow Center is a key
architectural component in the
comprehensive master plan for the Dallas
Fine Arts District. The tower is designed to
serve as the "campanile" for the district.
This analogy is reinforced by the tower's
cruciform shape and its classic
composition of a base, shaft and top.
The tower is set back from the street by
an extensive public plaza and two-story
entry pavilion which further integrate the
tower with the street and the adjacent,
lower-scaled cultural institutions.

The tower is clad in a combination of
polished and flame-cut autumn brown
granite and bronze reflective glass. Bay
windows rise at different heights on the
facade to a five-story sloping glass pyramid
which houses executive suites with
spectacular views of Dallas. The lobby, with
its three-story rotunda of white marble,
provides a focus for a Rodin sculpture.
The remainder of the lobby reflects the
axial symmetry of the cruciform floor
plan, with walls clad in panels of West
African rosewood detailed in bronze, and
a pattern of marble floor paving.

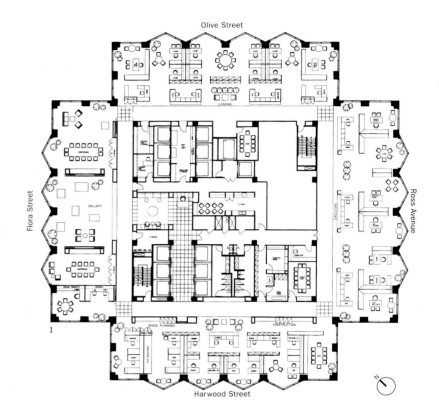

1 Typical floor plan
2 Dallas skyline
3 North facade

3

5

6

7

6    Elevator vestibule
7    North lobby
8    West lobby

9

10

11

12

# Texas Commerce Tower

Completion 1987
Dallas, Texas
Trammell Crow Company
Skidmore, Owings & Merrill,
Richard Keating, Design Partner
1,400,000 square feet
Concrete poured in place
Granite, glass, cast stone

Designed as a companion building to
the Trammell Crow Center, this building
derives its basic form from its predecessor
yet maintains a distinct identity. The
55-story tower is clad in granite, rusticated
at the base and polished above. As the
tower rises, the granite gives way to glass
forming a giant opening, the building's
predominant skyline feature. The
opening, or sky window, is 75 feet high,
27 feet wide, and 80 feet deep, and
separates floors 41 through 49. At floor 50
the gap is bridged, providing full floors
above the sky window. The floors on either
side of the opening provide approximately
9,000 square feet for tenants requiring less
space but wanting prime views.

1

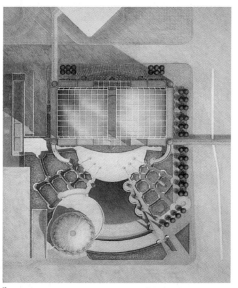

2

1   Detail at base
2   Site plan
3   Tower view

3

4 Entry vestibule
5 Base and garden
6 Fountain
7 Pedestrian entry

4

5

6

8

8  Banking hall
9  Skylobby

## The Wilshire Buildings

Beverly Hills, California
Columbia Savings & Loan
Skidmore, Owings & Merrill,
Richard Keating, Design Partner

Four buildings were designed along
Wilshire Boulevard, two of which were
built, two of which remain as fully
documented designs. Three of the
buildings, located east to west at
Robertson Boulevard, La Peer Boulevard,
and Elm Street, were conceived as a trilogy
of buildings for Columbia Savings & Loan.
A fourth building at Canon Street, facing
the heart of Beverly Hills' retail district,
was designed for different purposes.

1

2

3

The sites for the Columbia Savings
buildings are on the south side of
Wilshire Boulevard, several blocks apart.
The predominant influence on the
architecture is the boulevard itself which,
as a major thoroughfare, is experienced
primarily from the automobile. To the
motorist, what is perceptible is the rhythm
of the street wall and the edges of
buildings. The Columbia Savings buildings
have individual character but form a
unified concept. Coloration, scale, and
composition vary but the basic premise
remains consistent—facades made up of a
set of planes organized on an expressed
structural frame.

1   Wilshire La Peer/ICM Headquarters
2   Wilshire at Elm
3   Wilshire at Cañon

## Wilshire at Robertson

Design 1986
Beverly Hills, California
Columbia Savings & Loan
Skidmore, Owings & Merrill,
Richard Keating, Design Partner
75,000 square feet

The building planned at the corner of
Robertson and Wilshire acknowledges
both the terminus of the plane of
limestone which binds the three buildings
together visually, and the shift in angle of
the street at the corner. Using a rotunda,
about which passing cars would negotiate
the bend in the road, the building serves
as an eastern anchor for the triad.

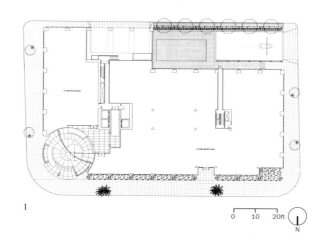

1

0    10    20ft
N

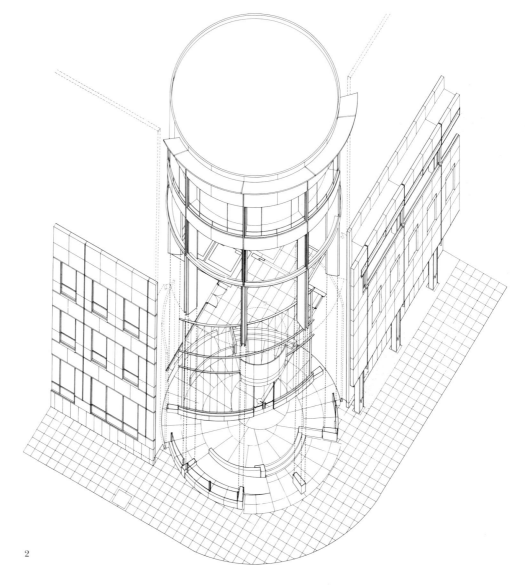

1  Plan
2  Axonometric corner entry

2

## Wilshire La Peer/ICM Headquarters

Design/Completion 1986/1989
Beverly Hills, California
Columbia Savings & Loan
Skidmore, Owings & Merrill,
Richard Keating, Design Partner
82,000 square feet
Steel frame
Limestone, granite, steel, glass

The building was originally planned as the centerpiece of the triad of Columbia Savings buildings, and is highly articulated and texturally rich. Lifted above the street level, the facade creates an uninterrupted edge to Wilshire Boulevard, supporting the continuity of the thoroughfare, yet allowing visual and functional permeation into a courtyard and offices beyond. Its design is based on the characteristics of its construction, with an exposed copper-clad structural frame and layers of Indiana limestone. The expanse of the limestone is interrupted by stainless steel supports and circular forms that emanate from the geometry of the courtyard. With the corners left open, the structure serves a dual purpose of providing views down the boulevard from within and defining an articulate edge for approaching motorists.

*Continued*

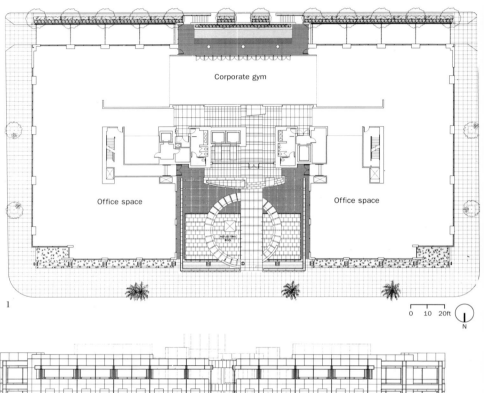

1

0   10   20ft

N

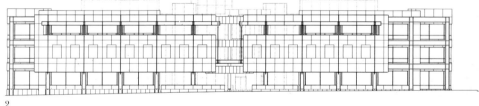

2

1   Plan
2   North elevation
3   Entry courtyard

The courtyard provides a transition from the traffic and movement of the street. The almost symbolic front door and grand scale of entry is achieved by organizing interior circulation as part of this space so that each user of the building is visually and functionally associated with the courtyard. The paving, fountain, and black pyramid (by artist Eric Orr) are all designed to inhabit the space and provide a focus into the courtyard. At the interior entry of the building, Indiana limestone, flamed-finish green granite, and stainless steel are combined with figured maple to connect the architecture with the interior.

4

5

6

7

## Wilshire at Elm

Design/Completion 1987/1990
Beverly Hills, California
Columbia Savings & Loan
Skidmore, Owings & Merrill,
Richard Keating, Design Partner
54,000 square feet
Steel frame
Limestone, granite, steel, glass

The Wilshire at Elm building is located six
blocks west of the ICM Headquarters
building and marks the western boundary
of the building trilogy. It is a simpler
exploration of the principles used in the
ICM building but continues the limestone
plane with its fragmented rhythm of
substance, excavated space, and structure.
While the gestures are less extravagant
here than in the headquarters building,
a close examination reveals great attention
to both the detailing and the engineering
of details.

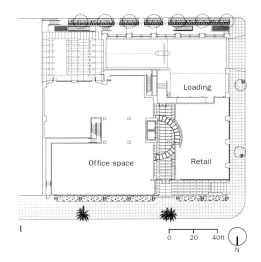

1

0    20    40ft

N

1   Plan
2   North elevation
3   Street front

2

3

4

5

6

4   Entry
5   Lobby
6   Lobby
7   Entry canopy detail

## Wilshire at Cañon

Design 1988
Beverly Hills, California
Columbia Savings & Loan
Skidmore, Owings & Merrill,
Richard Keating, Design Partner
90,000 square feet

The project site is at the diagonal intersection of Wilshire Boulevard and Cañon Street. Responding to the distinct character of each street, the design combines a rhythm in the structural configuration that is comprehensible from passing automobiles along Wilshire with a tranquillity in the facade as viewed by pedestrians on Cañon Street.

The front wall is recessed from the street under a canopy of architectonic elements and behind a precisely designed garden. The part of the facade which curves out to meet the diagonal alignment of the site with Cañon Street was planned as a focal point for the project, to incorporate the glass coatings and technology of artist James Carpenter. The garden is conceived as papyrus emanating from a perfect black granite plinth. It is in counterpoint to the building line and is periodically interrupted by linear void spaces corresponding to the building's structural rhythm.

1

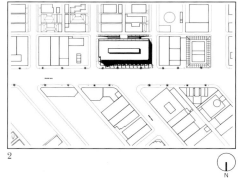

2

N

1  Street front
2  Site plan
3  Axonometric

3

4

4 Partial elevation
5 Facade and landscape model
6 Wall section detail

5

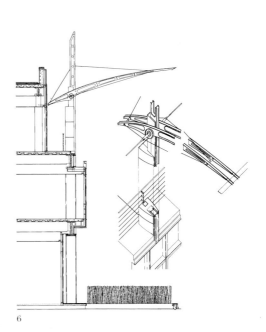

6

# Sun Bank Center

Design/Completion 1983/1987
Orlando, Florida
Lincoln Property Company/Sun Bank
650,000 square feet (office tower)
98,000 square feet (park building)
Skidmore, Owings & Merrill,
Richard Keating, Design Partner
Poured in place concrete
Precast concrete, glass, aluminum

The entire development project encompasses a full block in downtown Orlando. Its character derives from an understanding of the beautiful quality of daylight in central Florida. The materials and details respond to the context of the region as well as a concern for budget and construction. The lattice which is used as a formal element at both the very large and very small scale—even into the interior of the bank—creates a cohesion between each of the components and manipulates the play of light throughout the day. A light granite was used for the tower, while detail elements, including the smaller office building, are all precast concrete.

*Continued*

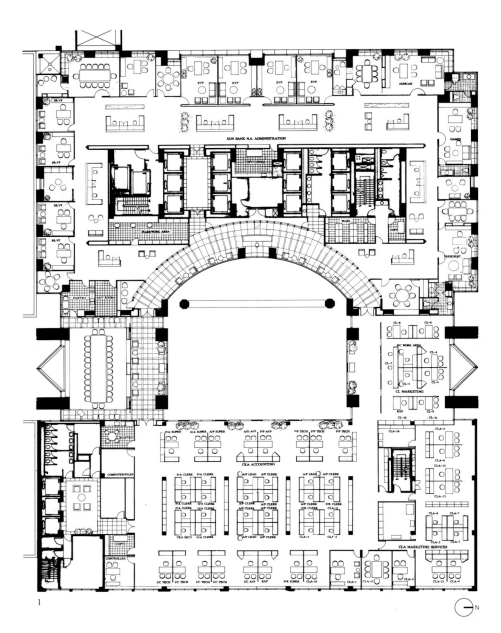

1

N

1  Plan: new tower and existing building
2  South view

2

3

4

5

6

The existing seven-story Sun Bank building remained in operation on the prime corner of the site throughout the design and construction process and was ultimately joined to the new tower to create large, useful floors for the bank. A seven-story atrium space connects the older building to the new tower and provides a dramatic banking hall and signature space. Additionally, a seven-story park building screens the garage from view.

The interiors of Sun Bank occupy approximately 350,000 square feet on 11 levels of the new tower and renovated building, as well as 29,000 square feet of dining facilities in the park building. Levels 4 through 8 bridge the existing building and tower, giving each of the levels efficient floor plates of 35,000 square feet.

7

8

9

7  Executive dining
8  Cafeteria
9  Executive office
10  Executive reception

# Pacific Atlas

Design 1988
Los Angeles, California
USA Pacific Atlas
34-story tower, 55-story tower,
550-room hotel
Skidmore, Owings & Merrill,
Richard Keating, Design Partner

The site for the Pacific Atlas project consisted of an entire block of downtown Los Angeles between the central business district and South Park, an area which has long been targeted for revitalization. The proposed project included two office towers, a hotel and a public park.

The organization of the site plan is based on a pair of crossed axes—the primary axis running parallel to the street grid and the secondary axis shifted at an angle to the first. The relationship between these axes is the foundation for the architectural and functional decisions. The buildings are placed accordingly, with the 34-story tower at the southwest corner, the 55-story tower midblock on the east side, and the hotel occupying the whole of the north edge. Together these elements create an internal urban park, the public focus of the project. Formal access to the site occurs in two places at points where the two axes meet the perimeter.

*Continued*

1

2

The architecture of the 34-story tower, designed for Phase I, reflects the underlying premise of the site plan. The influence of the primary axis is evident, but the disruption caused by the displaced axis is more emphatic. The north elevation is at a right-angle to the primary axis, while the south wall is pushed out to the angle of the secondary axis. In response to the freeway, from which motorists would see the building for only a few seconds, the south facade is an easily perceived, graceful curve of green glass, scaleless except for a large window revealing the angle of the primary axis inside. The north facade, which is seen from downtown and the park below, is sliced by an arc and appears to reveal layers beneath the outer wall.

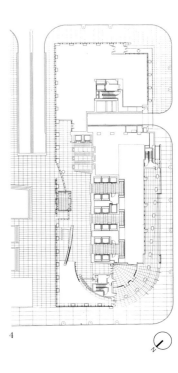

4

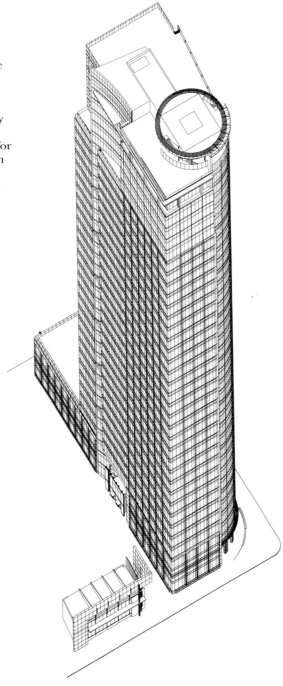

3

3   Plan
4   Site plan
5   West elevation
6   Aerial view
7   West view, 55 story tower, Phase II

5

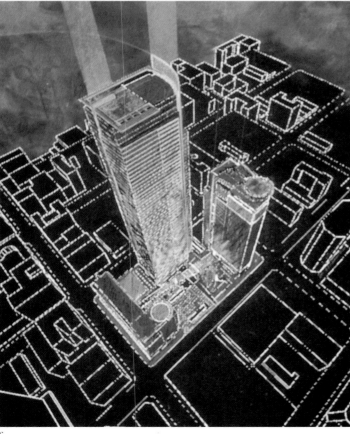

6

7

# Stockley Park Competition

Design 1988
London, England
Stanhope Properties, Ltd
Skidmore, Owings & Merrill,
Richard Keating, Design Partner

The Stockley Park office building, outside London, England, proposed a sense of urbanity within the openness of its suburban setting. A long, low-rise plan was chosen to minimize the building's impact on the surroundings and to provide continuous views from within.

Landscaping defines the character of the project, integrating it into the natural setting and providing a transition from surroundings to building. A tree-lined road approaches the area, crosses a stream and passes through a semi-circular portal into the site. The planting along the road then becomes more formal, culminating in a garden court in front of the building. Here the landscaping is highly refined with plants, flowers, and water combined with works of art to create an elegant outdoor room.

*Continued*

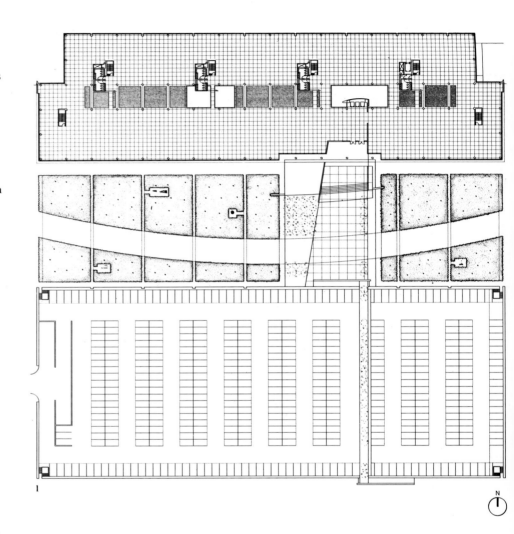

1   Plan
2   South elevation and entry

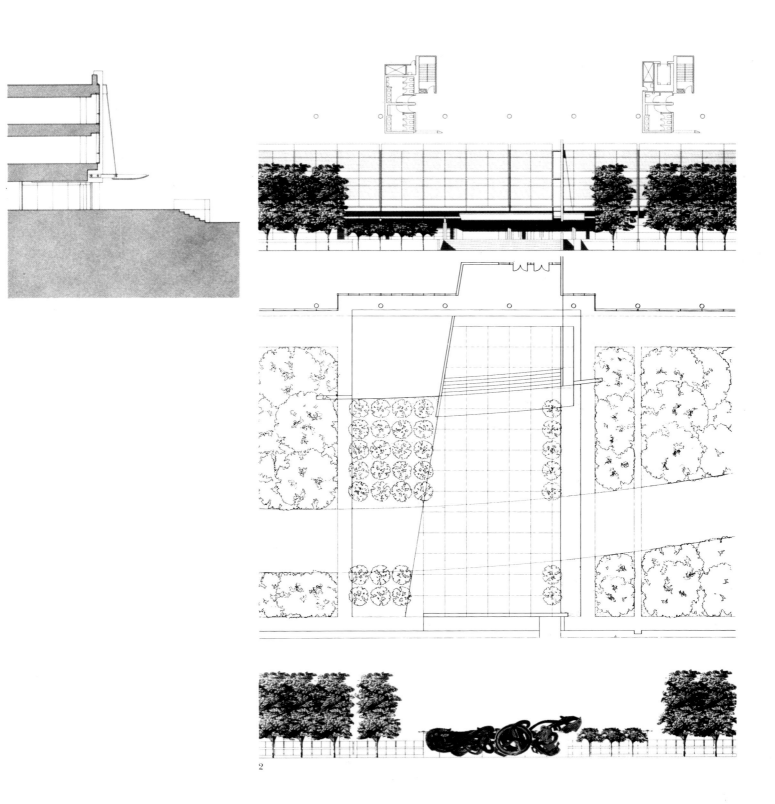

2

A simple plan of two floor plates 60 feet wide, separated by an atrium 30 feet wide, provides the greatest possible floor area for interior functions. Uninterrupted areas of easily divisible space organized around private offices, and the utilitarian functions of the ceiling grid, allow maximum flexibility. The atrium is a linear, sun-filled space crossed by bridges connecting the floors. Landscaping in the interior space is in the form of trees hanging in pots from the ceiling, evoking a Magritte painting.

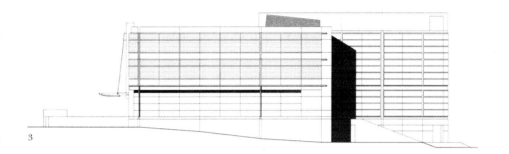

3

4

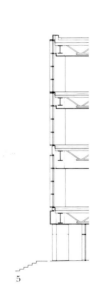

5

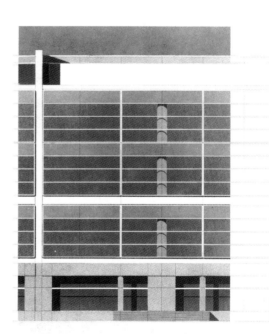

3   East elevation
4   North elevation
5   South elevation at entry
6   Section
7   Atrium, planter detail
8   Axonometric

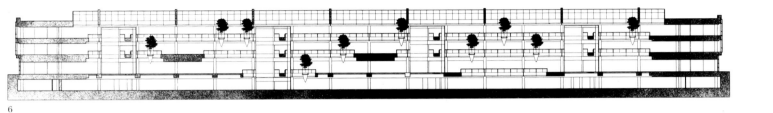

6

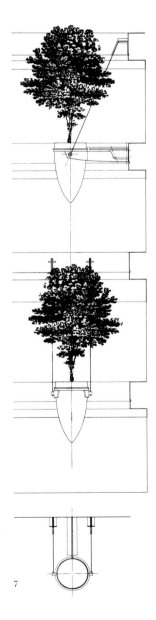

7

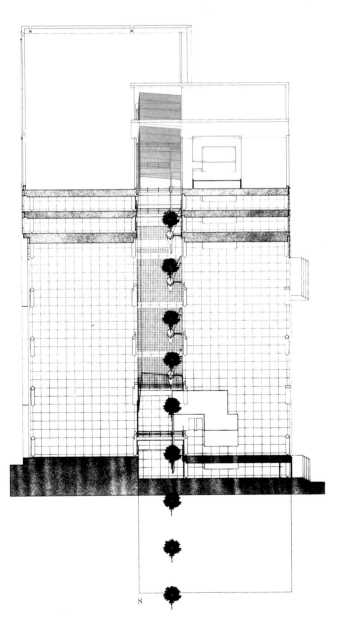

8

## 3rd at Mission

Design 1988
San Francisco, California
Wells Fargo/Crocker Properties/Hines Interests
Skidmore, Owings & Merrill,
Richard Keating, Design Partner

To accommodate the very real and precise needs of Wells Fargo Bank, this scheme is based on a functional plan. The building's character recognizes San Francisco's architectural heritage without compromising the modern construction techniques or the needs of the user. It also recognizes its larger contextual role as a corner building in relation to now-completed adjacent buildings. The fenestration attempts to work within the recurring construct of vertical rhythm and careful scaling that is prevalent throughout the city. Accommodating 350,000 square feet of floorspace and a courtyard of historic gold rush iconography, it would have been a major cultural and business gateway to the downtown.

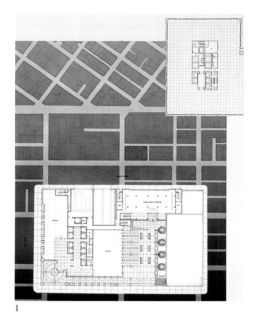

1

2

3

1   Site plan
2   South elevation
3   Museum court
4   West elevation

# Aichi Corporate Headquarters

Design 1988
Tokyo, Japan
Aichi Corporation
68,000 square feet
Skidmore, Owings & Merrill,
Richard Keating, Design Partner

This corporate headquarters building was designed for a location on the south side of Shinjuku-Dori, one of Tokyo's major streets. The 18-story, 68,000-square-foot tower is set within a garden to provide a buffer from the chaos of the street. The building plan consists of two dislocated squares, juxtaposed onto a nine-square grid. It accommodates the maximum floor area allowed on the site while meeting Tokyo's complex zoning ordinances regarding shadows cast onto the street and surrounding properties. To achieve this, computers were used intensively to test and adjust the building's dimensions, height and placement on the site.

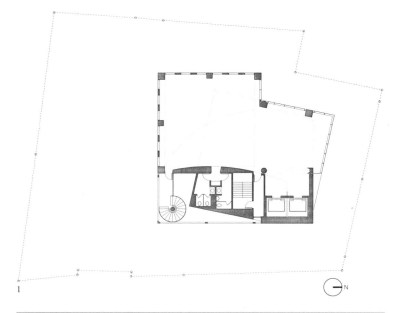

1

2

3

## Solana Marriott Hotel

Design/Completion 1987/1989
Westlake, Texas
Maguire Thomas Partners
180,000 square feet
Skidmore, Owings & Merrill,
Richard Keating, Design Partner
Walls: integral color plaster, some with figured cherry wainscoting; Verde
Tinos marble; Asahi "rice" glass
Millwork: figured cherry veneer; acid-washed bronze; polished Andes
granite;
Paving: Arizona sandstone with patterns of polished Andes granite,
French limestone and gray Spanish limestone

The Solana Marriott Hotel challenges the
image typically associated with a business
hotel. Its architecture is bold and colorful
and, while responsive to the hues and
vastness of the Texas prairie, is unlike any
architecture in the region outside the
Westlake campus. The interior was
designed to complement the strong form
and color of Ricardo Legorreta's exterior
architecture, while introducing a level of
detail and texture important in creating
an intimate environment for the
individual guest.

The architectural language is established
by the stone wedge and curved ceiling
element at the main entry, the
asymmetrical cone over the bar, and the
columned, vaulted pre-function area.
With varied textural finishes and a rich
color palette, the resulting environment is
one of distinctly separate spaces unified by
glimpses of one from another. The
diversity of interior spaces reinforces the
architectural concept of sequential
discovery and surprise rather than
immediate comprehension; some are lively
and dramatic, others contemplative and
simple.

*Continued*

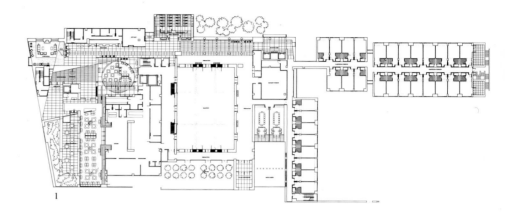

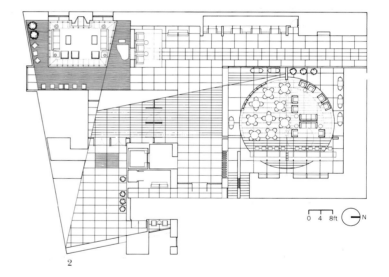

1   Plan
2   Public area plan
3   Entry

3

The hotel bar was designed as a dramatic space. There, the ceiling is formed by an asymmetrical cone rising 40 feet and topped by a glass oculus. During the day, sunlight fills the room, playing on the variety of patterns and brilliant colors used for walls and furnishings. At night the ceiling is like a telescope filled with stars.

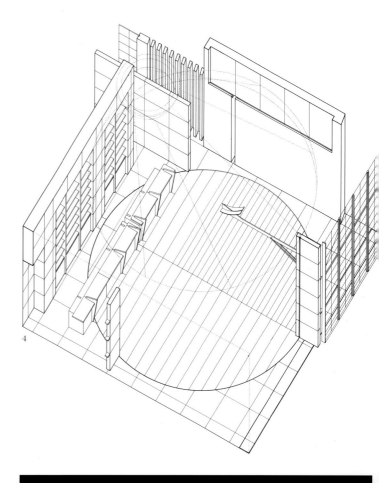

4

5

6

4   Axonometric lounge
5   Light detail
6   Lounge
7   Typical room plan
8   Reception

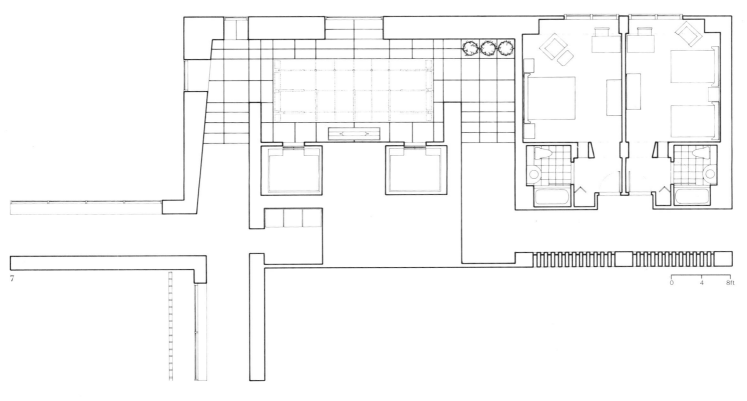

0   4   8ft

# American Honda Headquarters

Design/Completion 1988/1991
Torrance, California
American Honda
800,000 square feet
Skidmore, Owings & Merrill,
Richard Keating, Design Partner
Steel frame
Precast concrete, glass

The 100-acre site for the American
Honda Headquarters was designed
as a linear campus; buildings and parking
are organized by a pedestrian spine
extending the length of the site. The
double-height lobby of the administration
building straddles the spine while the
700-foot-long, two-story service shops
(the Technical Center) define one edge.
A 15-foot-high retaining wall extends
from the administration building to
provide a base for the two-story data
processing facility.

The buildings total 800,000 square feet
of floorspace and share a similar
aesthetic, characterized by textured
precast concrete panels combined with a
tinted glass and metal window system.

1

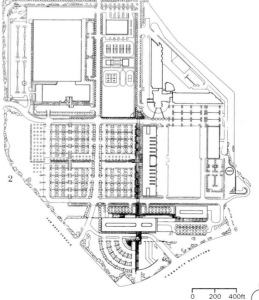

2

1  Shop facility and headquarters entry
2  Site plan
3  Data Center
4  Data Center
5  East elevation: headquarters and computer
   buildings

# Gas Company Tower

Design/Completion 1988/1992
Los Angeles, California
Maguire Thomas Partners
Skidmore, Owings & Merrill,
Richard Keating, Design Partner
1,750,000 square feet
Aluminum and glass curtain wall; Barre Grey
and Lanonline granite stone cladding

This 55-story tower is a compact,
street-defining form that rises up to a
boat-shaped blue glass volume intended
to evoke the official symbol of the Gas
Company. Most of the curtain wall is based
on a 5-foot panel unit without corner
joints that is quick to erect and appears
seamless.

The steep site has been used to create
a series of interlocking lobbies whose
monumental scale is relieved by retail
spaces, canted screens, and an internal
window that provides views of the park
for visitors descending the escalator.

The company cafeteria and other public
spaces are located in a low-level section
that protrudes from the base of the tower,
anchoring the building firmly on the
narrow site and reinforcing the lower scale
of adjacent Pershing Square. A slot left
over to the north was treated as "borrowed
space" for the main lobby and embellished
with a block-long mural by Frank Stella.

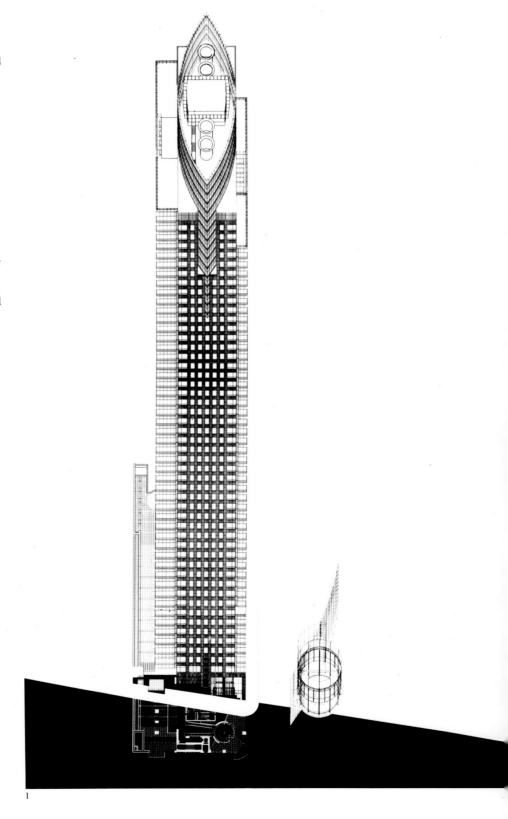

1   Axonometric
2   View from Pershing Square

1

82

3

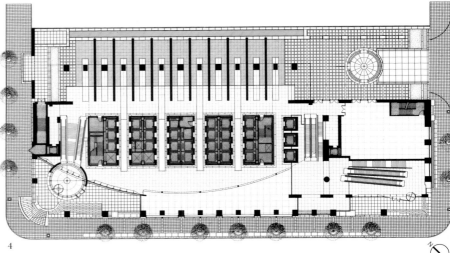

4

5

6

8 Lobby: view from the east
9 View through lobby to fountain and mural

8

# British Petroleum Plaza

Design/Completion 1990/1992
Houston, Texas
British Petroleum
480,000 square feet
Concrete
Precast concrete, glass curtain wall

British Petroleum Plaza is located at the extreme western edge of Houston, Texas. The building is oriented north–south, creating a dominant image from the adjacent freeway and providing a clear view and orientation to downtown Houston on the horizon. This orientation is further marked by the gesture of the stainless steel canopy at the building top.

The base of the building extends beyond the tower to accommodate the need for larger floorplates and houses data processing, the cafeteria, and the employee fitness center. A glass-walled, air-conditioned pedestrian link connects the garage to the office tower, providing weather protection and views to the landscaped courtyard.

The lobby interior is minimal, focusing on the richness and texture created through the combination of glass, wood paneling and stone. BP Plaza is uncomplicated in form, balancing the need for maximum efficiency inside with an appropriate outward aesthetic of conservative elegance and quality.

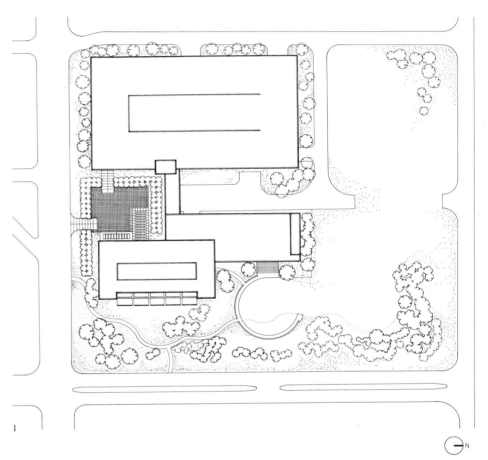

1

N

1   Site plan
2   Entry court
3   East view

2

3

4

4 Entry
5 Plan
6 Detail at entry
7 Pedestrian link

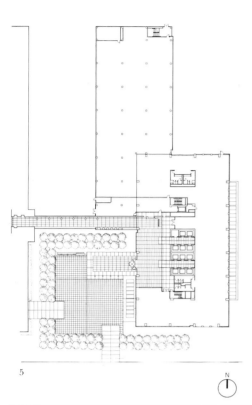

5

N

6

7

8 Lobby
9 Lobby: view to elevator banks
10 Pedestrian link and lobby

9

10

# BMC Software Headquarters

Design/Completion 1991/1993
Houston, Texas
BMC Software Inc.
600,000 square feet
Steel-framed structure; concrete shearwall lateral system;
post-tension beams with 42-foot column-free spans
Precast concrete, glass

The new BMC Software Headquarters building is based on deceptively simple elegance and form integrated into a complex landscape and site development. The site is bordered on one side by a freeway and on the opposite side by single-family homes. The future development of an additional one million square feet on the site was a further consideration.

The scheme adapts the front yard/back yard arrangement typical in suburban America to a corporate setting to achieve public and private spaces. The overall site is planted with deciduous trees, forming a grid with 40-foot centers. At the center of the site is a walled court which gives access to both the building and the visitor parking. Inside the court the landscape changes to a more precise urban setting organized at the pedestrian scale. The scale is emphasized by a stand of perfectly spaced indigenous evergreen pine trees set into a shallow recess in the center.

The space within the court allows for a wide variety of meeting and gathering experiences and casual dining, and will be a central feature in future phases of development.

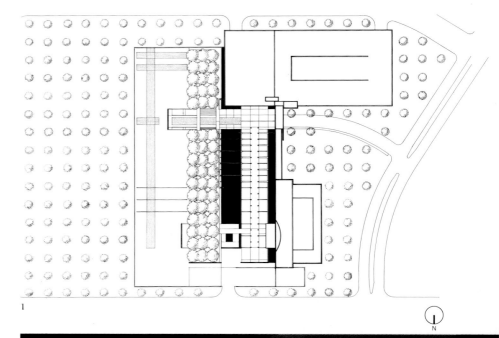

1   Site plan
2   Site model
3   East facade

3

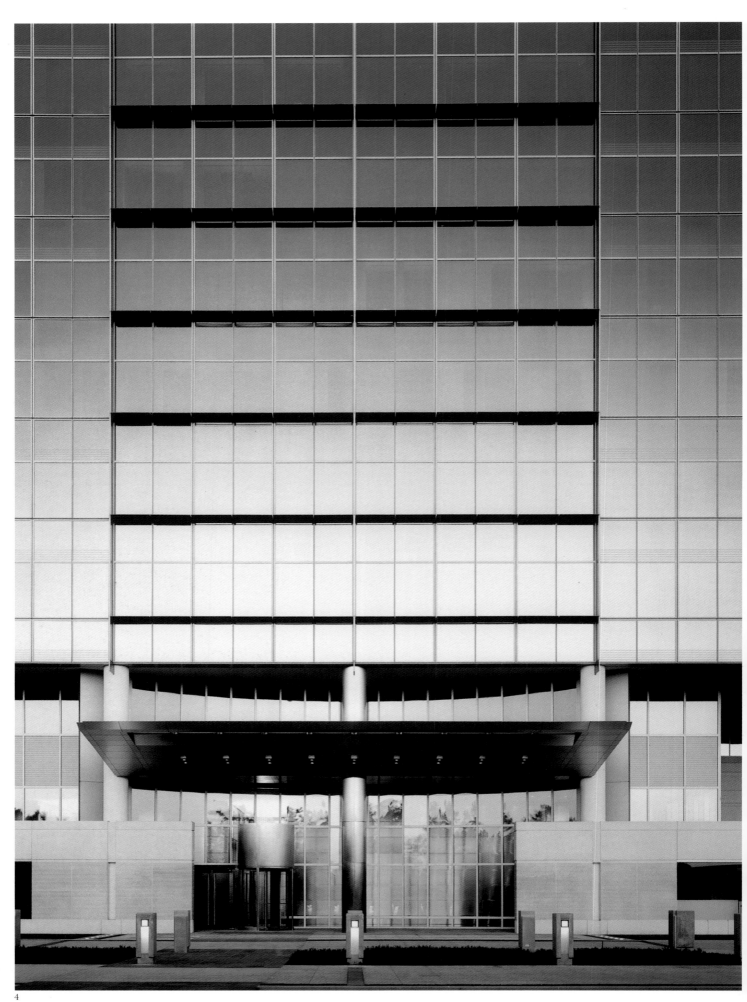

4

5

7

8

9

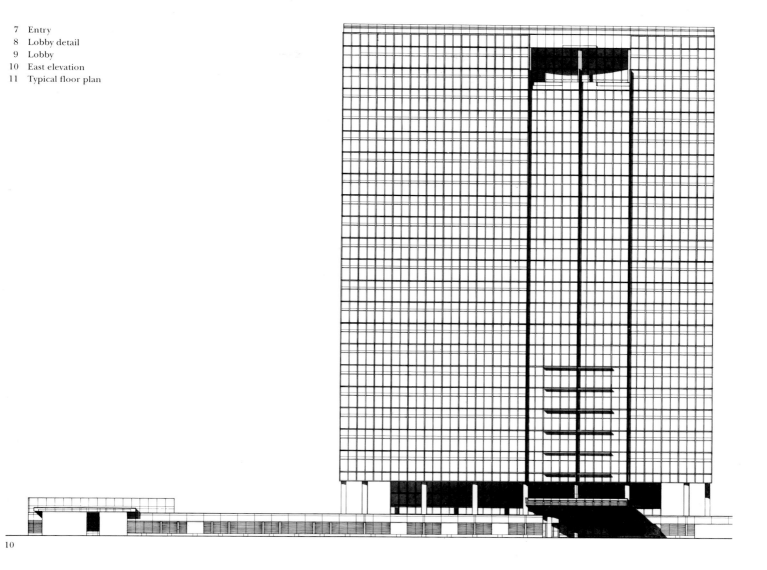

10

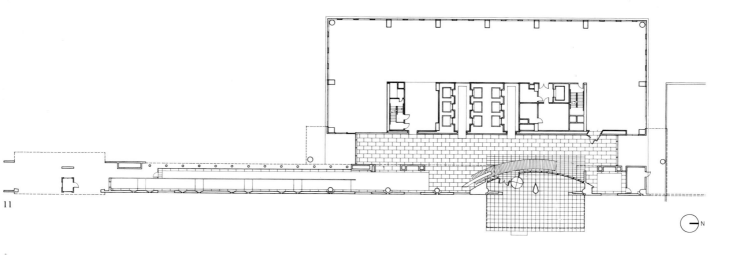

11

# Opel-Kreisel Office Building

Competition 1994
Frankfurt, Germany
Georg von Opel
312,163 square feet
Glass, dichroic glass, steel

Because of its location and proximity to major roadways, the Opel-Kreisel site provided a significant opportunity to create a major new office building which was also a visual gateway to the city center. The scheme is a direct response to these site conditions.

The subtle, curving facade of reflective glass is both a landmark and an elegant termination of the row of buildings along the Theodor-Heuss Allee. The facade is interrupted by inset concave bay windows that serve as a counterpoint to the large wall while offering extraordinary views to the surrounding area.

The elevator and service core is constructed from poured-in-place concrete with mechanical louvers and openings in metal, providing a sculptural contrast to the glazed curtain wall.

The Franklin Street wing is carefully scaled to respond to the adjacent buildings in height, fenestration, and materials. Its mass is relieved by a large opening that provides views across the park immediately to the north.

1

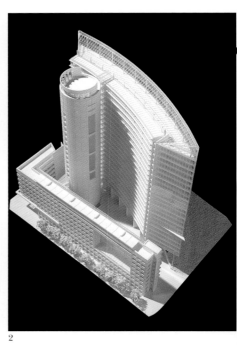

2

3

4

1   Facade, north view
2   East view
3   East view
4   South view
5   Theodor Heuss–Allee facade

5

# Hewlett Packard Business Center

Design/Completion 1993/1995
Atlanta, Georgia
Hewlett Packard Company
600,000 square feet
Concrete frame
Precast concrete, glass, steel

The Hewlett Packard building site is in
a suburb of Atlanta, Georgia where the
terrain consists of rolling hills and lush
vegetation. The master plan uses the
topography of the site together with new
landscaping to create a precinct for the
office tower, successfully shielding the size
of the development from the lower
sightlines of adjacent residences.

To accommodate the sizeable parking
structure required, the hillside was
excavated so that parking and specialized
computer areas could be placed partially
under ground. The deck top over the
parking structure is landscaped to create
a garden at the southern, formal entry to
the building. The building frames the
longer view to the sky and treeline beyond.

The richness of the architectural
expression is attained through the
manipulation of the facade to
complement the scale of the garden side,
rather than the larger scale of the freeway
and surrounding neighborhoods.

*Continued*

1

1  South facade
2  North view
3  East view

2

102

4

Furthermore, the unique large-scale elements of the Hewlett Packard program—the cafeteria and computer facilities—are placed outside the main building to provide an optimized configuration for each of their specific functions. While the computer facilities are buried from view, the cafeteria offers employees a distinct change from the office environment. Facing the garden and outdoor dining terrace, the entire room is bathed in natural light from above.

5

6

4  Lower courtyard
5  Upper courtyard
6  Parking structure detail
7  Pedestrian link

8

9

8    Lobby
9    Dining terrace
10   Pedestrian link

106

11

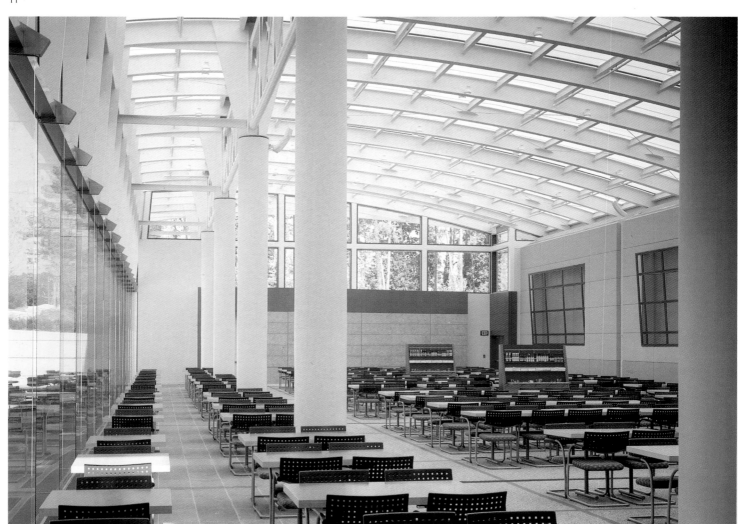

12

13

# International Center

Design/Completion 1993/1997
Dallas, Texas
Harwood-Pacific
Phase II: 215,000 square feet
Phase III: 200,000 square feet
Plaza: 50,000 square feet
Building: precast concrete, glass, granite, aluminum
Plaza: precast, glass, granite
Lobby: glass, granite, copper

The site plan is organized so that each building is associated visually and physically with a substantial garden and fountains. The buildings rigorously adhere to demands of efficiency and flexibility—simple rectilinear structures with maximum lease space, structural systems, service cores, and mechanical systems—but with a level of detail and finishes typically associated with larger buildings. Parking is hidden from view beneath the plaza as is truck loading.

The focus on the plaza provides a unique natural environment for daily office activity, in contrast to most downtown Dallas office environments.

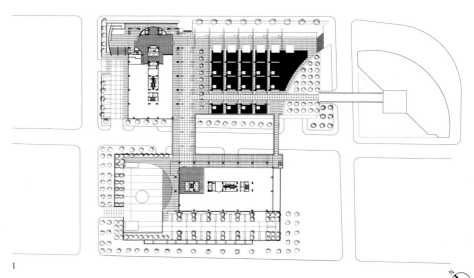

1

2

3

This type of project is equal part strategic intervention, urban planning, and corporate design. Each building requires a clear understanding of what is deficient and what is possible. As a designer, it is important to understand that a pre-existing building has a kind of "genetic code" that needs to be dealt with in any redesign effort. Equally important is the understanding that the designer's satisfaction may come from a success at problem definition/problem solving as much as from visual character.

# Renovation/Rehabilitation

# Tenneco Employee Center

Design/Completion 1979/1982
Houston, Texas
Tenneco Realty Inc.
Skidmore, Owings & Merrill,
Richard Keating, Design Partner
100,000 square feet
Steel
Metal cladding, glass, granite

The Tenneco Employee Center is an addition to the top of a parking garage, designed to house health and dining facilities. The two-story, 100,000-square-foot addition features indoor gardens, dining rooms, an audio visual center, and a fitness center, all designed to create a peaceful contrast to the office environment.

The exterior of the parking garage was remodeled to complement the original Tenneco Building designed in 1963, using painted metal cladding and bronze-tinted glass. Sunset red granite, which was used on the original building, was incorporated into the exterior design of the Center and throughout its interiors.

The main employee dining room on the lower floor opens onto a 250 x 45 foot garden which runs the entire length of the building. The planting and water displays are rhythmically arranged to provide a pleasant environment and visual focus for the separate dining areas, which are connected by granite walkways.

1

114

2

3 View before remodeling
4 Exterior
5 Garden wall interior

3

4

# Renaissance Center

Design/Completion 1985/1989
Dallas, Texas
Prudential Insurance Company of America
Skidmore, Owings & Merrill,
Richard Keating, Design Partner
1,650,000 square feet
Structural steel frame
Blue, silver and green insulated glass curtain wall

Built in the early 1970s, Renaissance Center enjoyed a prominence on the Dallas skyline, but over time was surpassed in quality and image by newer buildings developed around it. Aesthetically, the building had a strong identity only at night through its double-X patterned night-lighting; during the day, it was nondescript. Inside the building, materials were dark, dated, and worn, and the circulation lacked clarity. The building also had no street presence, unremarkable and undefined entries, and a lack of human-scaled elements.

The design approach was to address the functional issues of systems upgrades while at the same time correcting image problems that had contributed to an inability to attract and retain tenants.

*Continued*

1

1  Dallas skyline
2  Before renovation
3  South view

2

118

3

A subtle pattern of glass drawn from the blues and greens found in the surrounding skyline gives the new facade richness and rhythm, breaking up the massiveness of the plane walls. The familiar double-X light patterns were incorporated into the new design through the use of varied colored glass in the curtain wall, so that the pattern was visible during the day as well as at night. The large grid pattern follows the intersection of the column lines and the diagonal bracing, establishing a sense of scale and creating further visual interest.

*Continued*

4

5

4　Partially reglazed
5　Skyline
6　Tower and pyramid

6

A glass pyramid, added to provide a dramatic entryway within the plaza, also houses a dining facility. Rooftop spires were added to the building, featuring an intricate 160-foot-high central pinnacle surrounded by four corner spires. These graceful structures add height and elegance to the building's image. In the evening they are bathed in beams of light, brightening downtown Dallas.

7

8

9

10

11

12

13

14

11  Elevator lobby after renovation
12  Elevator lobby before renovation
13  Lobby before renovation
14  Lobby after renovation

# First National Bank San Diego

Design/Completion 1988/1993
Equitable Real Estate
580,000 square feet
White Cippilino marble with stainless steel inlay;
Roche De Cry limestone; blue pearl granite;
flamed impala granite; Verde Issore marble;
figured maple; frosted glass

Originally completed in 1982, the
Columbia Center (as the building was
formerly called) was designed to
accommodate a variety of tenants as well
as the First National Bank of San Diego.
The building also had three levels of retail,
designed to complement the City's
original plans to build its convention
center adjacent to the building.

The building's problems were typical of its
genre—dark materials and finishes which
showed the effects of 10 years' use; non-
compliance with current code regulations;
as well as changes in use over time. The
lobby had been planned to give maximum
access to the original three levels of retail,
and included an unnecessary escalator.
Since the need for the retail element had
disappeared, the configuration of the
lobby was inappropriate for its actual use.
The circulation through the lobby was
confusing and cluttered, a fountain
separating the parking garage shuttles
from the building elevator lobbies.

*Continued*

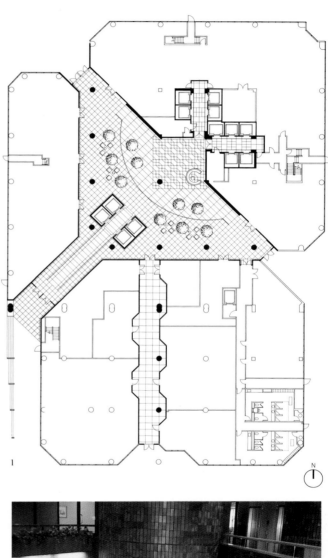

1

N

2

128

Entry from the street was also confusing. The building had five street entries but none served as the formal main entry. Since the completion of the building, the city had developed in the opposite direction to that predicted, leaving the token "front door" facing the wrong side of the property. The building had been set into a sunken walkway in order to achieve the maximum number of floors while remaining within zoning height limitations, and this caused all entries except one to be down a set of steps. That one entry was subsequently redesigned as the formal main entry.

*Continued*

4

4   Lobby
5   Elevator vestibule

The design team began by taking their cues from the building's blue reflective glass, prow-shaped atrium, and views of San Diego Harbor. Without applying a nautical theme literally, the concepts of natural light and a sparkling glass facade were central to the redesign. On the ground floor, the fountain and escalator were removed to simplify circulation. Dark finishes and materials such as glazed brown brick pavers, rippled oak paneling, and mirrored ceilings were replaced with lighter (literally and perceptively) and more elegant materials. The existing bridges that spanned between the elevator lobbies were also "lightened," creating the effect of one large atrium instead of two smaller atria.

6

6   Entry before renovation
7   Entry after renovation

# 10960 Wilshire Boulevard

Design/Completion 1993/1995
Los Angeles, California
Hines Interests Limited
534,000 square feet
Sunset red granite (existing), stainless steel (canopies), French
limestone, wood, textured glass

This project is a renovation and modernization of a 20-year-old, 23-story office building located in a prominent area of Los Angeles. The client's goal was to completely remake the image of the building as a first-class, contemporary business environment by enhancing functionality, aesthetic appeal, and tenant service orientation. The modernization included asbestos abatement, updating of all life-safety systems, and conformance with California's Title 24 and national ADA requirements.

Specifically, the renovation addressed public areas of the building, including building entrances and main lobbies, the multi-tenant common space on each floor, and the retail arcade linking the building to the garage, as well as extensive landscaping and refilming of the exterior facades. Most of the original driveway area was given over to landscaping to create a garden-like setting which became the primary design intervention, giving an entirely new character to the building.

*Continued*

1

134

2

The predominant concepts guiding the lobby redesign were to create a strong link between the garden entry and Wilshire Boulevard and to create a lighter lobby interior. While maintaining the existing sunset red granite cladding of the walls, a complementary palette of French limestone, carpets, natural wood, and textured glass was added. The existing bronze lobby storefronts were replaced with clear glass. With the new materials and the increase in natural light produced by the clear glass entries, the lobby takes on a warmer, richer, and more open character. To alleviate the existing confusion regarding access from the garage, a new gallery cuts through the ground floor, directly linking the garage and lobby.

Incorporating the natural wood and carpets of the main lobby, the elevator cabs and floor lobbies serve as transition zones to the typical floor corridors, where different levels of finishes are used. The corridors themselves were recarpeted, painted, and given new ceilings and lighting. The typical floor bathrooms were completely redone with new tiles, lighting, fixtures, and granite counter tops.

The building's exterior facades were refilmed using two brighter films: a soft silver film over most of the building, with two large vertical bands of soft bronze film running from each of the two entries to the top of the building where they are terminated with new canopies. The use of the two film types gives the building a more elegant, vertical proportion which, along with the canopies, provides a new character when viewed from a distance or from the adjacent freeway.

3

4

3  North facade
4  Exterior entry: view to lobby
5  Building lobby: prior to renovation
6  Elevator lobby: prior to renovation
7  Elevator lobby: after renovation
8  Building lobby: after renovation

5

6

7

8

# Houston Industries Plaza

Design/Completion 1988/1996
Houston, Texas
Houston Industries
1,100,000 square feet
Steel, diagonally braced frame
Granite, glass, stainless steel

The transformation of this building for Houston Industries is a unique exercise in architecture, rehabilitation, and city building. Built in 1972, the existing building's neutral facade and straightforward floor plan created a timelessness and efficiency that eludes some buildings of the 1980s. Over the years, however, the relatively elegant and simple flush curtain wall has been allowed to deteriorate into a patina of chalky discoloration. Moreover, the original concept of a base subordinated to retail under a glass skirt had been a failure, and the building suffered from the lack of a clear entry. The circulation pattern leading to the elevators was confusing and inappropriate for a first-class office building. The materials of the plaza, lobby, and public spaces were inappropriate for a building which must project a corporate identity.

The redesign creates a symbol of the light company on the Houston skyline that is effective 24 hours a day. This "lantern in the sky" provides screening for mechanical equipment and is complemented by a 70-foot-high light tower on the plaza.

*Continued*

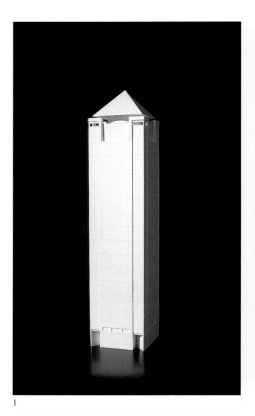

1

2

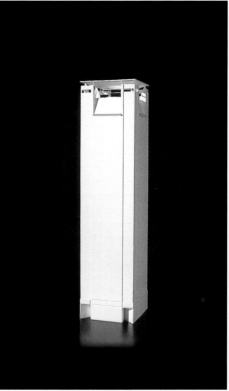

3

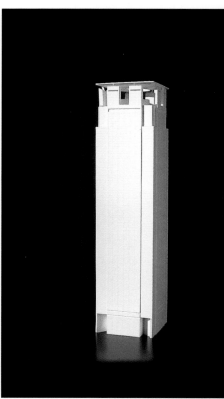

4

1–4   Studies
  5   During reconstruction

The light tower is a streetscape element of significant scale, which typifies the continuing efforts of our practice over the past 20 years.

The skin of the tower has been completely transformed, as have the base of the building, the internal circulation, and the lobbies, while the structural system has been upgraded, asbestos has been removed, and handicapped access has been improved.

The external expression at the base not only reflects corporate solidity, but also works with adjacent urban elements and spaces including the corner plaza across the street and its Dubuffet sculpture, the Tenneco Fountain, the Allied Bank entry element, and the strong base definition of each of the surrounding buildings. The continuity of the urban landscape is enhanced on this block, which provides extensive seating as well as skylights into the pedestrian tunnel system below.

*Continued*

6

7

8

The redesigned building lobby transforms the previous confusing circulation pattern into one that unites access from the street, the tunnel level, and a bridge level, culminating in an indoor park at the second floor. The materials and details reflect the character of the corporation, present and future technology, and the focus on employee amenities. This project represents a unique opportunity to bring together needs and opportunities, timing, vision, and a fundamental alignment of a multitude of people and roles. In the end, a city benefits, a corporation is more viable, and design is uncompromised.

9

9   Tower before renovation
10  Model: view from north
11  Base entry prior to renovation
12  Light tower
13  Base and entry: night view

10

11

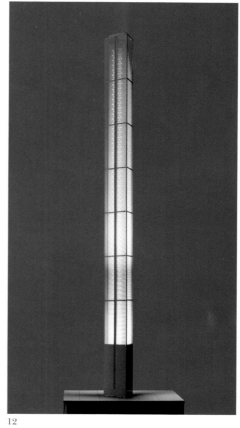

12

13

More than any other building type, architecture in the civic realm must seek to express the continuity, dignity, and permanence of our society. As such, the exterior character derived both from materials and from the public spaces associated with and enhanced by the building, become an extension of the general public's image of itself. It is in this area that the designs often make contextual transitions in character depending upon the situation. For instance, our design proposal for the Los Angeles International Airport, while functioning as a signficant regional gateway, also expressed and embraced the inherent technology of movement systems and aircraft. At the same time, it projects the imagery of the future of our forward-looking city.

Alternatively, the new additions to the Memphis Brooks Museum began as an acknowledgment of the existing 1917 building by James Gamble Rogers and its place in the affections of the community. As an exercise in functional redefinition, including the interrelationship with Overton Park, this building design acknowledges the technology of the time in which it was built while successfully extending the genetic character of the earlier building.

The public realm as defined by open space embraces and extends our collective understanding of our communal sense. As such it is the fundamental "glue" of our urban form and is the primary aspect of our civic design. The integration of landscape concepts, spatial definition, color, texture, and landscape is at the root of all our work but takes a dominance in civic architecture.

# Civic Architecture

# Memphis Brooks Museum

Design/Completion 1986/1989
Memphis, Tennessee
The Memphis Brooks Museum
40,000 square feet (new addition)
40,000 square feet (renovation)
Skidmore, Owings & Merrill,
Richard Keating, Design Partner
Steel and concrete
Precast concrete, aluminum

The program for Memphis Brooks Museum called for a major addition that would provide expanded gallery space, visitor services, educational space, staff offices, and improved facilities. There were three existing buildings of very different styles on the site: the original Neo-classical building designed by James Gamble Rogers, built in 1916; and two subsequent additions in 1955 and 1973.

In response to the challenge of adding onto a regional landmark, the new 40,000-square-foot, two-story addition was designed to complement the 1916 building while maintaining integrity as a modern building. The fenestration of the facade, design of the details, and choice of materials were all approached with respect for the beauty of the original building. However, contemporary elements reflect modern sensibilities and the needs of today's user—a grand hall for public functions, a restaurant with outdoor seating overlooking a park, and a dramatic entry with a metal grid for banners and signage.

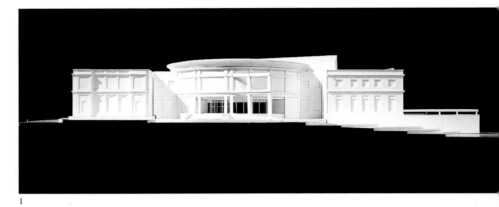

1

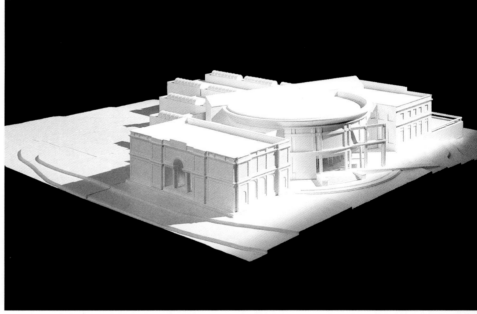

2

3

5

6

7

# Tokyo International Forum Competition

Competition 1989
Tokyo, Japan
Taisei Corporation
1,400,000 square feet
1,500-seat auditorium
5,000-seat grand hall
Skidmore, Owings & Merrill,
Richard Keating, Design Partner
Steel
Granite, stainless steel, glass

The design for the Tokyo International Forum was a response to the divergent character of the urban context, and an expression of the organization of a complex program. To the west of the building stand the regular blocks of the Marunouchi at a consistent height of 112 feet, creating an imposing wall of granite, stainless steel and glass. Beyond this lies the Imperial Palace, symbolic and impenetrable. In response to this context, the exterior of the Tokyo International Forum offers a monumental facade rising above the Marunouchi blocks, toward the Imperial Palace, and topped by a wing-like canopy. Significant is the visual penetrability of the structural frame which reveals the various functions of the building, including the stair tower which forms an inverted cone.

*Continued*

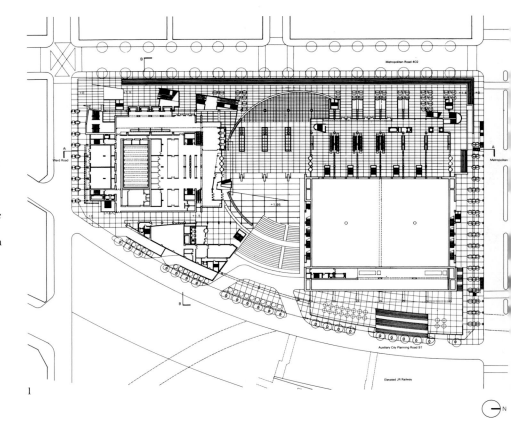

1

1   Site plan
2   Model

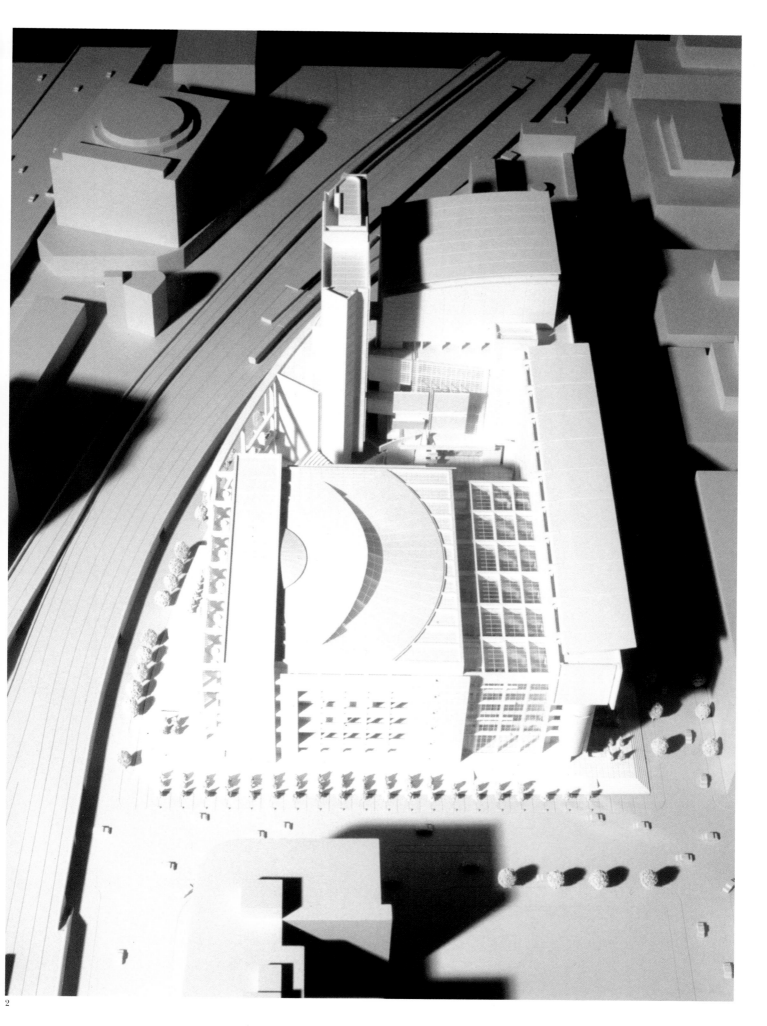

2

The intention was to facilitate circulation to the various uses of the building and extend a universal message of accessibility and the free exchange of ideas. The project was designed to accommodate the flow of many people arriving from all directions and at various levels. A central public court is the focus of the project and an important orientation point for visitors. Its character evokes the mass spectacle of the Shibuya Crossing, animated by video screens carrying images of the city, its culture, performances, and art.

The central court is flanked by two primary blocks into which the rest of the building's functions are divided for clarity. Conference rooms, reception facilities, a roof garden, and a 1,500-seat auditorium are located in the south block. The northern block houses a 5,000-seat hall with a roof of stainless steel and glass clerestory windows to let in natural light.

3

4

5

6

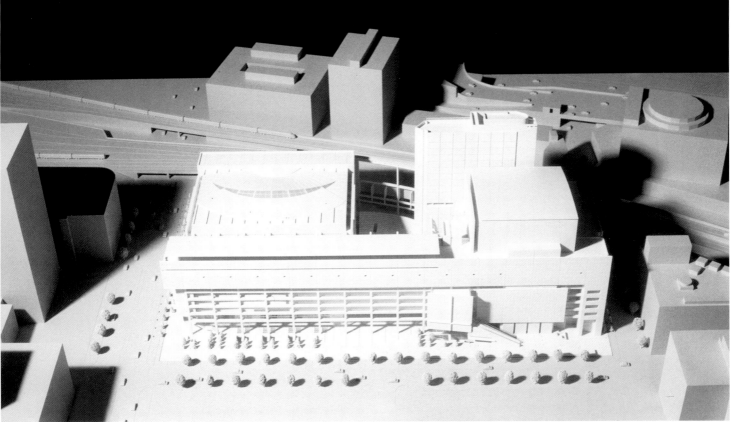

7

3 Maronouchi facade
4 Video court
5 South view
6 North view
7–8 West view

8

# Department of Ecology Headquarters

Design/Completion 1991/1993
Lacey, Washington
State of Washington
320,000 square feet
Steel-framed structure with a concrete shearwall
lateral system
Precast concrete, glass curtain wall

The site of this development is on a vast meadow at the edge of a dense forest, adjacent to a historic abbey and college. Because this building houses an environmental protection agency, an overriding criterion was that it be a model for future environmentally conscious office development. Materials and construction processes had to be ecologically sensitive.

The competition requirements stipulated a program of 312,000 square feet with surface parking for 785 vehicles. The scheme, however, challenges the guidelines, structuring the parking in order to preserve the meadow as an integral project component and symbol of purpose. The building is located at the forest edge on areas of existing root and soil problems. The building height respects the tree-line and screens the parking structure from view.

The building anchors itself to the "garden plane"—the landscape element extending from the entry court through the lobby and into the meadow. Rough fingers of stone mark the building entry, emerging upwards through the horizontal plane.

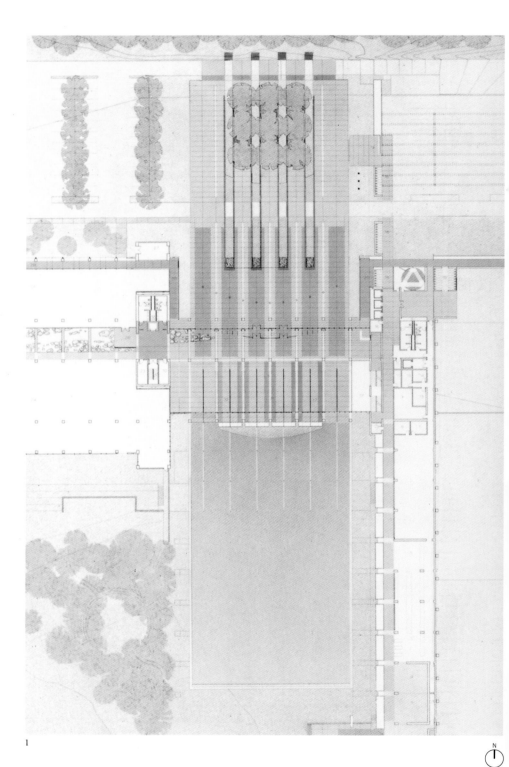

1

1   Entry plan
2   Main entry and fire stair tower at dusk

2

3

4

# Santa Monica College Library Expansion

Competition 1994
Santa Monica, California
Associate architect: Rotondi Architects
15,000 square feet
Wood slat and glass main enclosure

The existing campus of Santa Monica College is a compact group of buildings restricted from further expansion by the surrounding neighborhood. Two eras of construction activity on the campus are clearly observable in the orientation and scale of the buildings. The existing library occupies the center of the campus and essentially straddles the two underlying planning grids.

This proposed addition establishes both the physical and intellectual center of the campus while accommodating the grid collision. The predominant form of the library is the Oval Room, which is bowl-shaped with soft flooring to accommodate a range of seating possibilities. Above the room is an egg-shaped chamber intended as an area of total concentration and quiet.

The garden spaces outside consist of a trellised park with a bank of public telephones, and an academic grove that encourages students to take advantage of the climate and study out of doors. A controlled outdoor reading room located on top of a protruding wing of faculty study rooms provides a similar outdoor experience. The large screen above the symbolic building entry faces out toward the academic grove and campus, and offers numerous possibilities as a means of electronic communication.

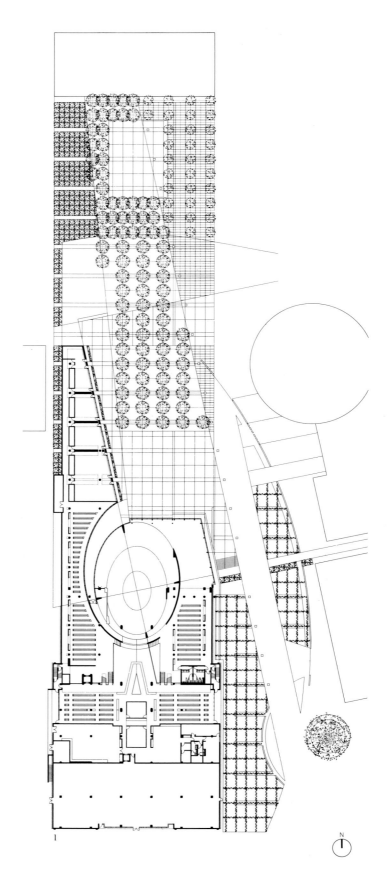

1

1 Site plan
2 Axonometric
3 Model

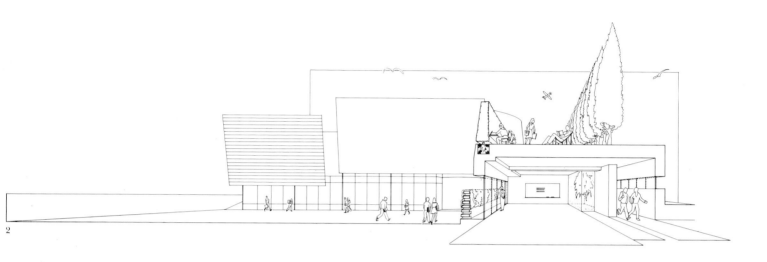

2

3

# San Bernardino Government Center

Design/Completion 1994/1997
San Bernardino, California
State of California
300,000 square feet
Steel
Precast concrete, glass, stainless steel

This initial scheme for the new State of California Government Center in San Bernardino includes two office buildings, a parking garage, and an extensively landscaped public plaza. The complex also includes a retail element at the ground levels of each of the buildings and garage. The overall goal of the City of San Bernardino and the State of California is to foster economic growth and revitalize languishing downtown areas. Therefore the project was conceived as a public place, providing amenities for users of the buildings and general downtown visitors.

The focal point is the public plaza which is lushly landscaped. Both buildings are entered from the plaza and from the streets which they border. The character of the buildings is civic and timeless and was driven by the State's modest budget and need for maximum interior accommodation. The image of the buildings is achieved through the fenestration and detail of the curtain wall of precast concrete and glass.

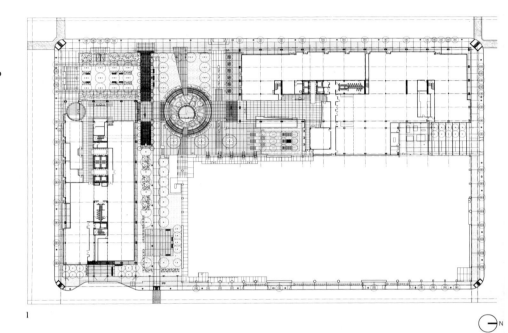

1

N

2

1   Site plan
2   West elevation
3   Illustration

San Bernardino Government Center   161

# Elihu M. Harris State Office Building

Design/Completion 1994/1999
Oakland, California
Dinwiddie Construction/State of California
700,000 square feet
Precast concrete, glass, aluminum, stainless steel

The aim of the State Office Building design is to maintain the functional imperative while respecting contextual issues to provide a design response that is clear from all angles—at the skyline, at the pedestrian level, and at the north and south facades. Of great concern was the development of a design that illustrated the stability and strength of the State of California while acknowledging the history and civic spirit of Oakland.

The distant perception is more dependent on form and the play of light and shadow. In this case the precisely sculpted top, with a distinct cornice line and horizontal gesture to the west, is unique on the Oakland skyline; but rather than being aloof and self-referential, it draws from the context and embellishes it. The perception of the building complex from a closer position is dependent on elements of scale, details, and materials.

*Continued*

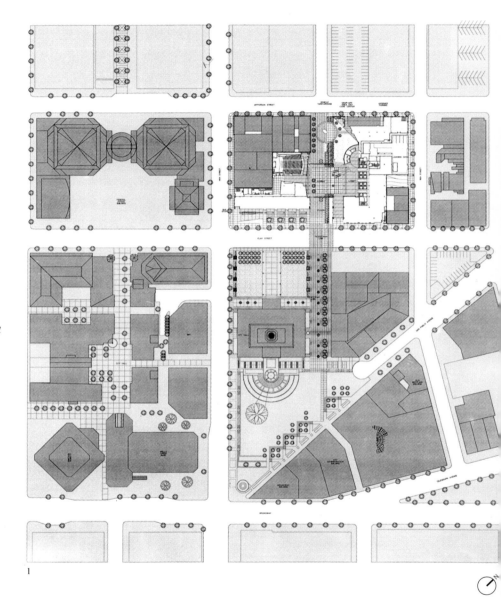

1

1   Urban context
2   Rendering: west facade

Elihu M. Harris State Office Building 163

The purpose of the landscaping and street amenities is to create a direct continuity with the Civic Square and City Center areas. Ultimately, the landscape design will help to integrate the adjacent buildings and provide a variety of vibrant outdoor environments for State employees and visitors to the State Office Building.

The facade of the State Office Building will be white cast stone, green and pewter glass, and charcoal mullions with stainless steel and aluminum details. The articulation of the stone and glass will be further enhanced by texture and shadow-lines. The appearance of the curvilinear cornice—the building's signature element—varies with the quality of light during the day: against the bright sky it is composed as a precise shadow and reveal; at night it is a unique source of light.

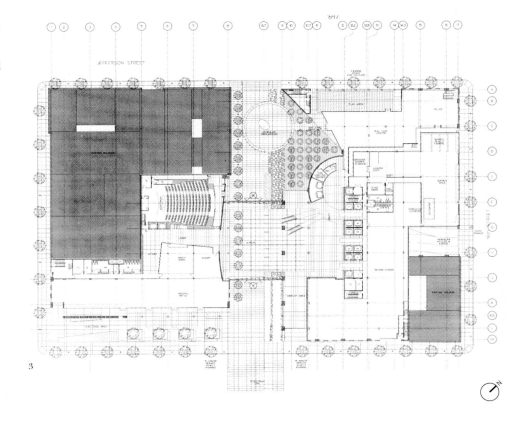

3

3   Ground level plan
4   Atrium

4

5

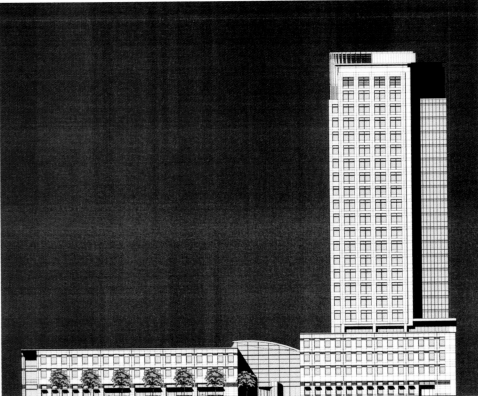

6

5    West elevation
6    East elevation
7    South elevation
8    North elevation

7

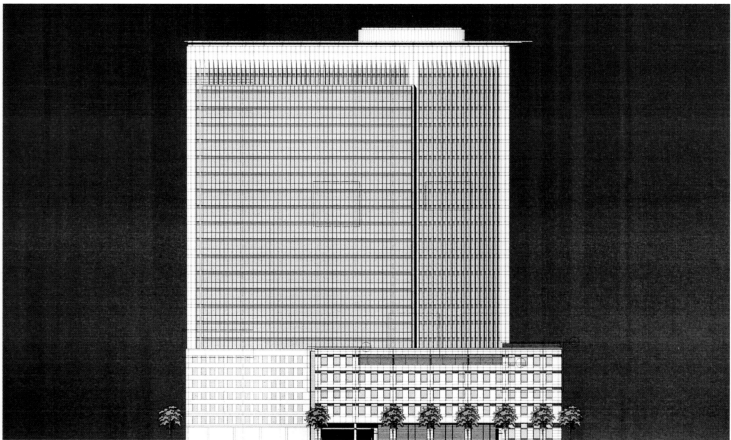

8

The larger scale of design that falls under the name of planning/urban design is fundamentally about how numbers of people perceive a place, and the strategic construct that will allow the character of that place to positively evolve over time while allowing for the vagaries of inevitable change. This is rarely about the design of a building or an object, but can be a strategic location or attitude about a building and/or a design of a pervasive armature to which the future evolution of development will be subordinated.

Landscape and natural settings can and always will play largely into the notion of armature. For instance, the strategic concept of Central Park in New York as a fully executed void space in an otherwise diverse urban milieu has been supported and enhanced over a century of evolution by the individual developments at its periphery. Similarly, the same can be said of the parks of Savannah, Georgia and Portland, Oregon; the boulevards of Paris, and the height restrictions of Philadelphia and Washington DC. The natural edges to which building activity is subordinated are exemplified by the San Francisco Bay, Chicago's Lake Michigan, and each Italian hilltown.

Our design has extended these notions of communally comprehensible space, or construct, and the wisdom of strategy and flexibility. This necessarily draws upon the existing fabric, whether rural land or urban context, in the belief that each construct is an addition to a setting that has been perceived communally and historically and will add positively to the future. The culture of man is fundamentally inherent in what we build and construct, and as such cannot be properly manipulated in individualistic terms.

In practice, this strategy has served to create an understanding of what is unique and crucial, whether an open meadow in the Department of Ecology building or a complete valley floor and river zone in a local suburban development. This most fundamentally involves the armature of the urban systems that weave private development together. Streets, often plotted and conceived in early urban history, are public vessels of activity that respond over time in successive redefinitions without necessarily changing their physical attributes. In downtown Los Angeles, or the center of Orange County, or the freeway exposure in Texas, the roadside strategy is subordinated to these vessels. With transit, what is critical is not necessarily the through passage, but the terminus and the potential of transfer and confluence. Both the Los Angeles International Airport master plan proposal and the Los Angeles Rapid Transit District Headquarters proposal involve the art and setting of human interaction. Cognitive public open space, whether the rural form of a river valley or the single remaining flatland property available for a park in Seoul, South Korea, is seen as having predominance over the built environment. Ecologically appropriate is almost always visually appropriate, and both are fundamental to man's history and future.

# Urban Design

# Tower City Center Competition

Competition 1989
Cleveland, Ohio
Tower City Associates
1,000,000 square feet
Skidmore, Owings & Merrill,
Richard Keating, Design Partner
Granite, glass

Tower City is a mixed-use development covering 10 square blocks between the core of downtown Cleveland and the Cayahuaga River, the city's natural boundary to the south and west. Phase III of the project includes Tower City Center, a 40-story office building of 1,000,000 square feet. The building is designed differently on the west and east sides to reflect its dual role as a part of the central core to the east and a symbol of new growth to the west. The tower's eastern facade is a curved, blue glass form which visually recedes into the expansive Midwestern sky. The curved wall, combined with a 300-foot-high spire on the top, gives the building extremely vertical proportions, reinforcing its role as a gatepost.

The project uses the river's edge as a major amenity by combining small harbors, residential towers, parks, and retail space.

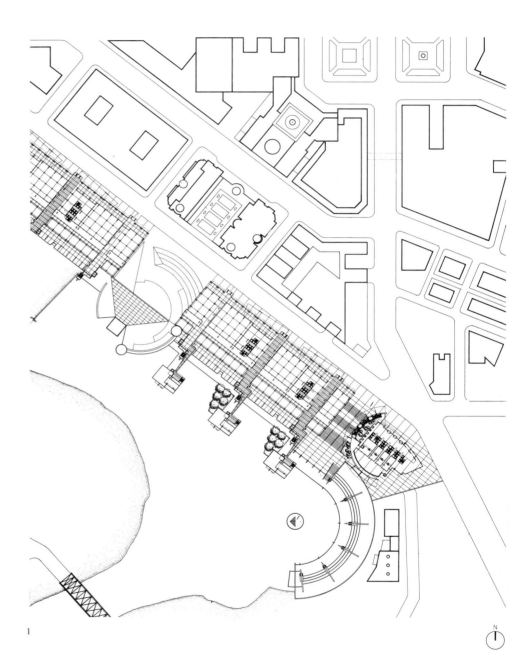

1

1   Site plan
2   Model: view from south

2

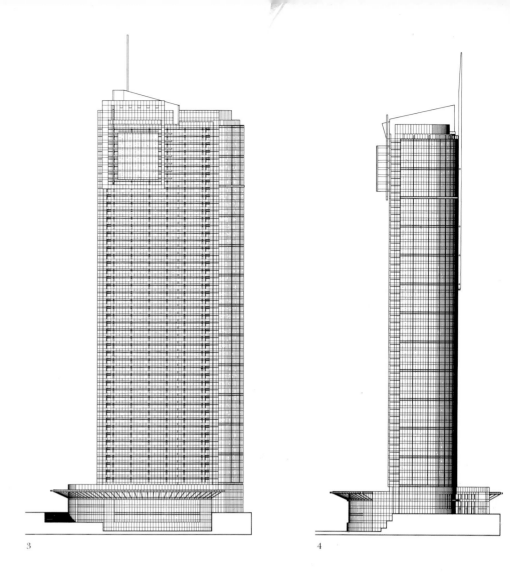

3

4

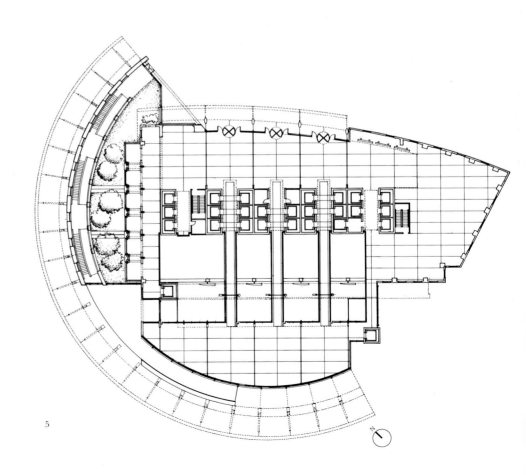

5

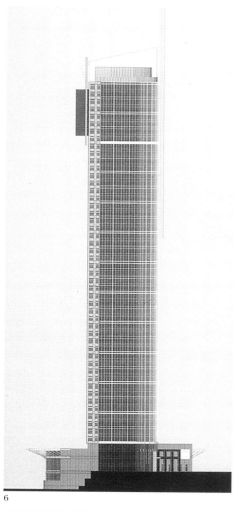

6

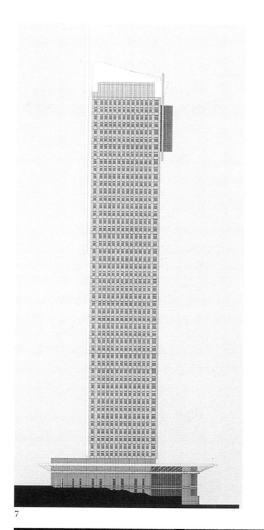

7

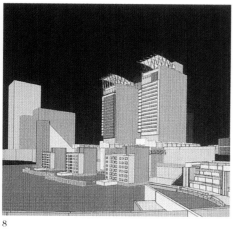

8

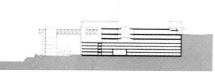

9

10

# Wilshire Ambassador Competition

Competition 1987
Los Angeles, California
Trump Associates
Skidmore, Owings & Merrill,
Richard Keating, Design Partner
2,500,000 square feet
Aluminum, granite, glass

The underlying concept of this scheme is to characterize the building as part of the natural continuum of Wilshire Boulevard, the linear corridor which is as much a symbol of Los Angeles as the Hollywood sign. Through the creation of an extensive garden, the open space is advanced as an important urban park. More importantly, through the addition of significant retail and elements of pedestrian activity, the design seeks to enhance the Wilshire corridor and introduce the kind of energy found in Times Square or the Shibuya District of Tokyo.

The building's shape, and its progress from base to the top, are logically integrated with functional and architectural criteria to allow for a continuous, efficient structural system. The lantern/helipad at the top not only serves structural needs, but also provides a beacon visible miles out to sea and far into the desert. The play of light through the slots in the upper part of the building and the gentle taper provide hourly drama across the elevations.

*Continued*

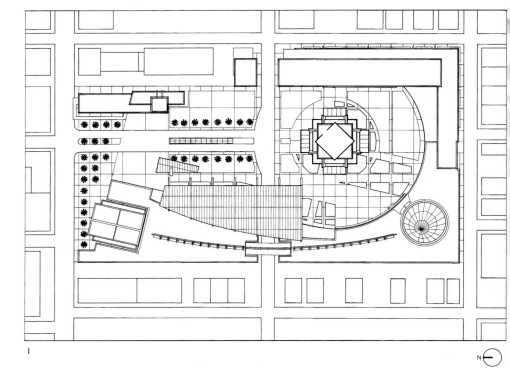

1

N

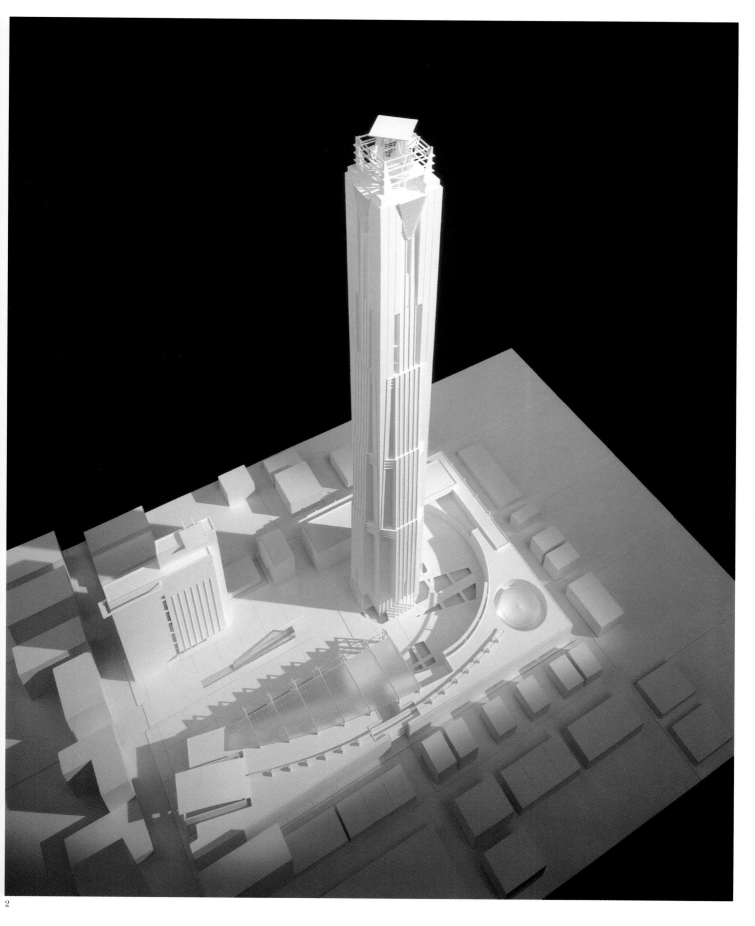

2

The structural system concept was determined on the basis of efficient wind-load resistance and considerations of occupant perceptions of motion during wind gusts. Additionally, the structural system had to provide adequate resistance and ductility to withstand strong seismic motion. The lateral stiffness for wind-load resistance is optimized by placing columns on the exterior of the shape and interconnecting them by means of vertical trusses. Apertures in the building provide substantial dampening of wind motion.

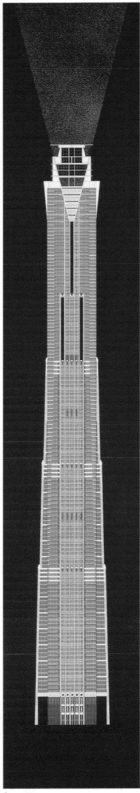

3

# Trammell Crow Center Irvine

Design 1989
Irvine, California
The Trammell Crow Company
Skidmore, Owings & Merrill,
Richard Keating, Design Partner

Within this large and significant site, which could become the centerpiece of an urban area, the strange geometry of the pre-existing building provided a clue to the ultimate formal attitude of the master plan. The master plan incorporates not only the existing building, but also the underlying platting or grid system of the surrounding and adjacent development, including "downtown" Irvine, the freeway, and the back bay ecology.

Recognizing the freeway frontage and its inherent associated imagery, an array of office buildings focuses on a transit stop which in turn becomes the central pedestrian hub of development. Parking for the office buildings, while above grade for economic reasons, becomes a retail frontage at the base and an enclosed form from the freeway, creating the central urban space. Future offices, housing, and retail extend from this space in a phasing strategy that provides flexibility, yet maintains the overall cohesive character for the development.

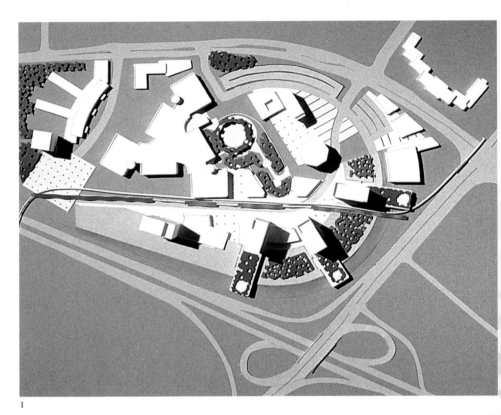

1

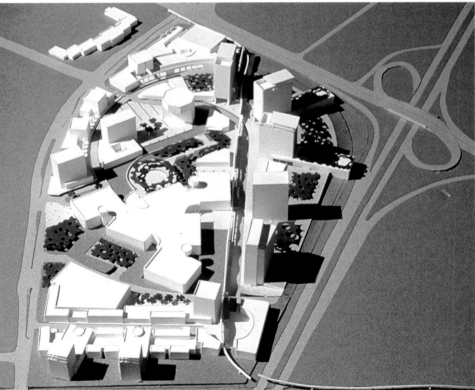

2

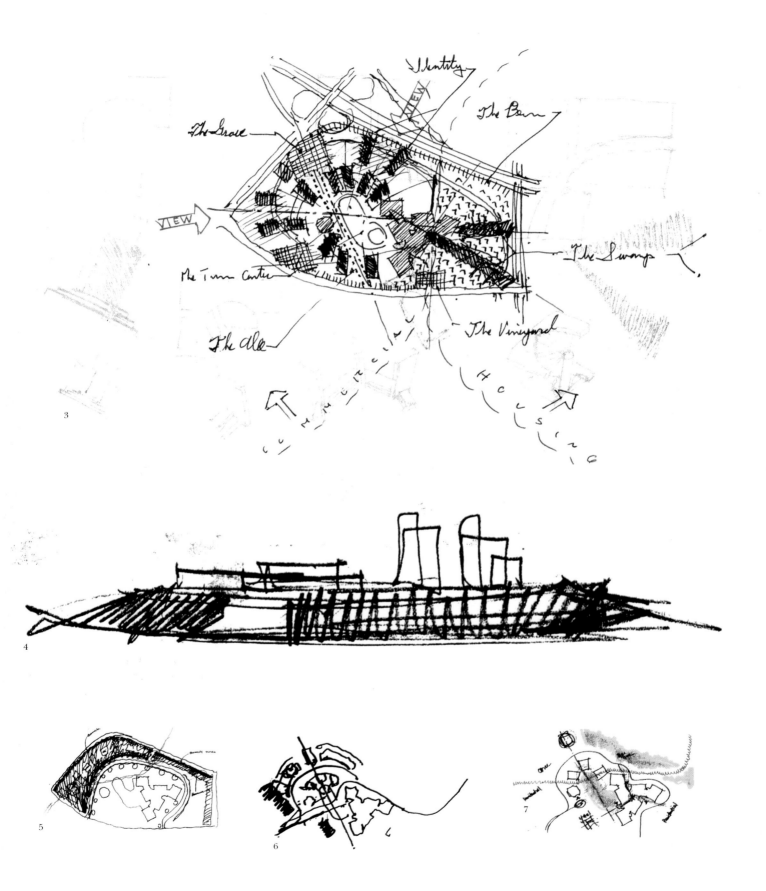

3

The Grove

Identity

VIEW

The Barn

VIEW

The Swamp

The Town Center

The Vineyard

The Ale

COMMERCIAL

HOUSING

4

5

6

7

## RTD Headquarters Competition

Competition 1991
Los Angeles, California
Catellus Development
600,000 square feet

This plan for the new RTD Headquarters building includes not only an architectural proposal, but also a reorganization of the entire master plan of the Southern Pacific railyards property.

To integrate the property into the larger city of Los Angeles and the adjacent downtown, two streets—Sunset Boulevard and Los Angeles Street—were extended into the property as the primary business addresses; the first by renaming existing streets, and the second by strategically bending Los Angeles Street into the depths of the property. This creates a primary public open space in front of the historic train station which would also provide a focus for the Olvera Street Market, binding together two currently separate but important cultural landmarks of Los Angeles.

A bus loop circles around another area of open space that slopes down to bring sunlight to the lower level train baggage arrival area and the transit line, organizing each mode of transit to a single point of confluence. The proposed transit company office building is located adjacent to this setting, creating a visual symbol of the transit systems and activities.

*Continued*

1

2

3

1  Urban context
2  Building and train shed
3  Freeway view
4  Train arrival

4

The architecture of the building expresses the technology of transit and is oriented towards the future. Placed at the edge of the property beside the freeway, the building would have exceptional prominence in the region. As the train museum would form the building's ground level, the historic trains would also be visible from the freeway.

An important opportunity was to enhance the primary arrival into Los Angeles by train and future high-speed rail. This was achieved through a dramatic Palm Court and train shed structure that would provide an important urban symbol.

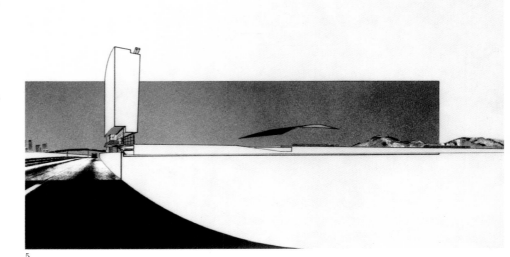

5

6

7

# Texas Rangers Stadium Competition

Competition 1991
Arlington, Texas
Texas Rangers Organization
12,000-seat stadium, 4,000 car spaces

The program for this project includes the Rangers Stadium, an adjacent Little League Field, a Hall of Fame, and an administration building. The special element of the project is baseball, and its role in American culture, both past and present. Expressed in vision, sound, smell, taste, and song, it is intertwined with a notion of summer afternoons and evenings, hot dogs and beer—a time when junk food is legitimate, and meaning and history are as important as the game at hand.

Wrigley Field and Fenway Park are revered as special ballparks, but their most distinguishing feature is that they are part of their surrounding urban fabric to a far greater extent than more modern stadiums which stand as isolated elements in an asphalt sea. This scheme sought to use the character of the Arlington urban form which is defined by its organization along the highway, the stadium itself, and large local amusement parks and their associated parking.

*Continued*

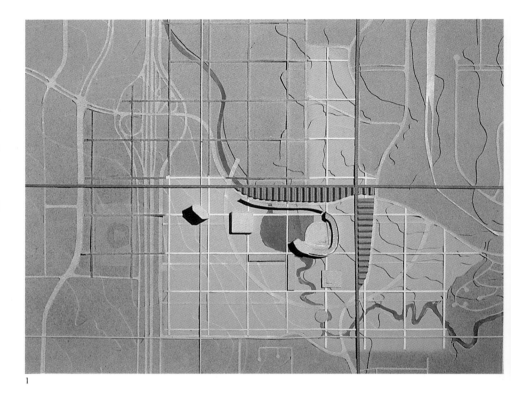

1

1   Context
2   Stadium and park
3   View from the north
4   Plan

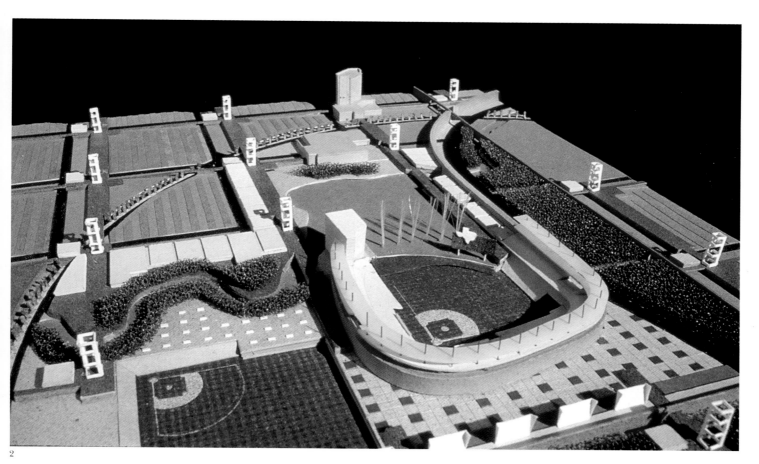

2

3

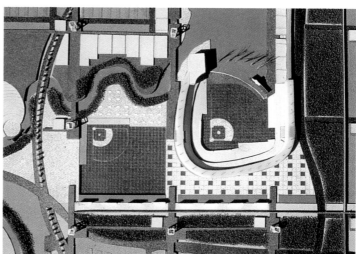

4

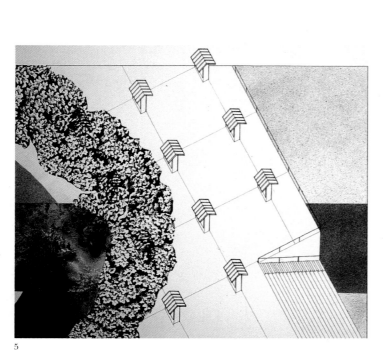

5

6

7

Parking lots at large entertainment venues are typically ignored, or are badly planned and disorienting. The proposed plan organizes the parking along the USGS survey grid, between landscaped pedestrian walkways which intersect at retail/restaurant/entertainment nodes marked by towers. These intersections of activity provide opportunities for revenue generation through sales of fast food, tickets, etc. As a counterpoint to this grid, the primary access road, the ballpark, and the Hall of Fame define their own geometry. The stadium design is focused on the movement of daylight across the colorful crowds and the transition from the late afternoon light of the early innings to the pitch black sky at the end of the game.

8

5   Food kiosks
6   View from the stands
7   Entry sequence
8   Little league field

# Los Angeles International Airport Master Plan Proposal

Design 1994
Los Angeles, California

This proposal would eliminate the upper level roadway that currently provides for departure drop-off, and which traps carbon monoxide fumes in the arrival area below. A large, semi-open trellis structure would envelope the internal area of the passenger zone, making a major architectural statement.

Extension of the terminal facilities would take place to the west, with a new international terminal overlooking the Pacific Ocean, itself a metaphor for the association Los Angeles has with other Pacific Rim countries of origin and destination.

The road system would extend to the beachfront. This would allow the volume of traffic between the airport and the Century Freeway to be doubled by looping traffic one way in and one way out. Truck and airfreight services can expand along the southern frontage where direct freeway access can be incorporated. The proposed subway transit system can be accommodated in a station and alignment down the center of the passenger area to accommodate those who arrive or depart by train in the same manner of efficiency and grace as other passengers.

1

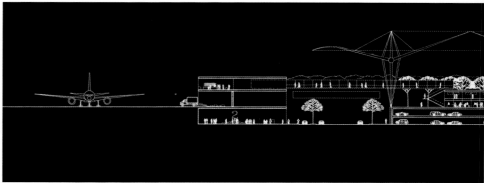

2

1 Plan
2 Section
3 View from the east

3

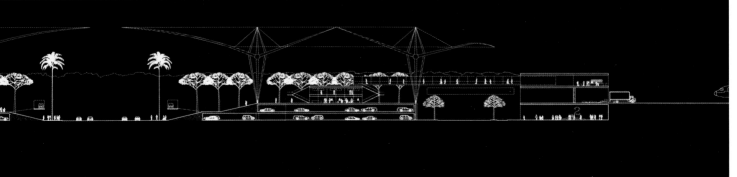

# Los Angeles Convention Center Transit Proposal

Design 1994
Los Angeles, California

A new convention center has recently been completed in Los Angeles, but due to a combination of factors including the lengthy construction period, the Los Angeles riots, and its location south of downtown, bookings have been less than expected. Current economics do not allow for the addition of a convention center hotel; even if they did, there would be a time lag of at least three years during its construction. While Los Angeles has a significant investment in its downtown, including the new Central Library, the Museum of Contemporary Art, restaurants, retail, and hotels such as the Sheraton Grande, the Hilton, the Hyatt, and the Bonaventure, none of these amenities is within a convenient distance or pleasant walk of the convention center.

This proposal recommends improvements to Figueroa Street through new street character, paving and design, landscaping and graphics, to improve the linkage between the convention center and the downtown core. The improved access would stimulate economic activity for downtown businesses as well as for the convention center. A specially designed bus—free of charge and open like a convertible—would capture the character of the car culture of Los Angeles and provide an icon not unlike San Francisco's cable cars.

This concept is part of a larger notion of accommodating the tourist trade, which is a substantial aspect of the region's economics. The bus system is unassailable as a 21st century image for Los Angeles, especially if it conveniently accommodates guests with a degree of panache and character.

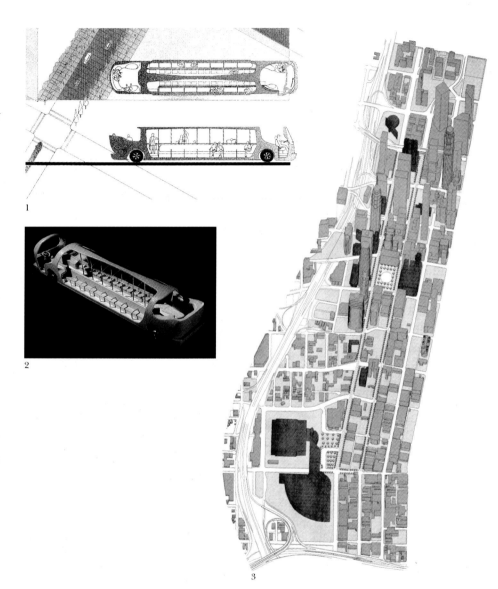

1  LA bus rendering
2  Model depicting typical layout of bus
3  Figueroa/Flower loop
4  Street character

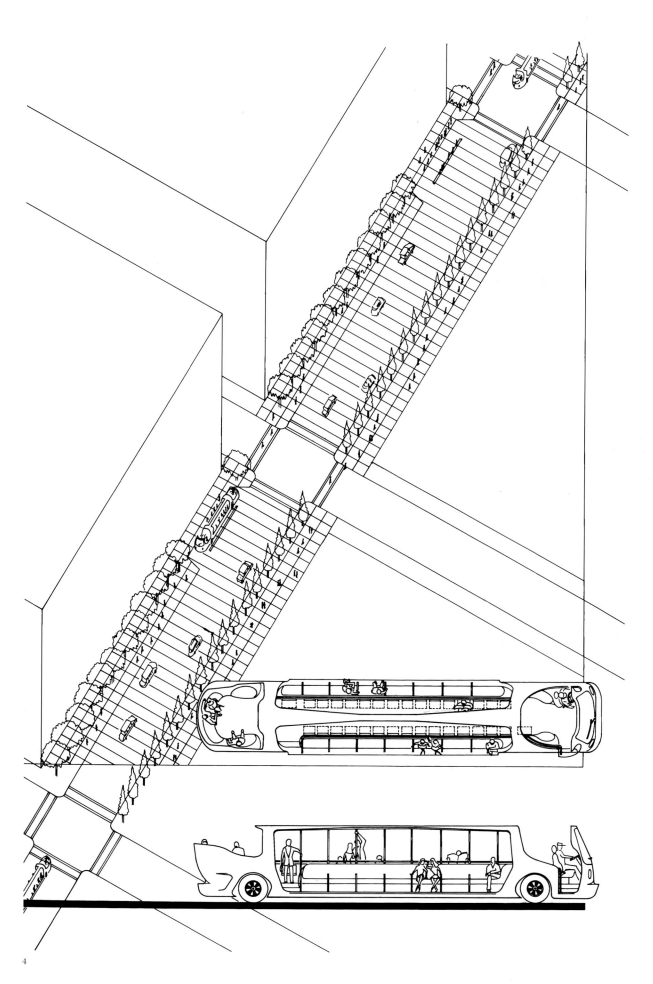

4

As a reaction to the pretensions that have evolved since the initial post-war simplicity in the design of single-family homes, the residences on the following pages have been based on an essential restraint. Seeking their logic from site conditions, each has achieved a modulation of interior space and sunlight without an overt loss of privacy. Span is dictated by optimum framing length, and form by the repetition of the spanning elements. The linear plan also allows for natural daylight from both sides. The individual spaces are left to flow around free-standing utility islands. In each case, the relationship to the garden and the exterior is paramount to living within. Additionally, the materials and detailing are emphasised to enhance the simplicity of the plan.

The ivy-covered walls of the Yoakum house fully screen the building from the street and the surrounding neighborhood, while the skylights and large corridors provide for abundant natural light to the interior. This house, more than the others, is not discernible from the exterior; it was designed as an internal space and accommodation for living rather than an object on view.

The Morgan house, while similar in plan, steps down the hill toward the entry sequence and garage at the lower end. The fenestration of this house adheres to the energy codes of Snowmass and is oriented toward the adjacent ski hill from which the entire length of the house is presented to passers-by through a veil of aspen trees. The Montecito house explores a variation on the plan, lifting the primary space, outdoor terrace, and lap pool to a point where clear vistas of the Channel Islands occur.

## Residential

# Morgan Residence

Design/Completion 1978/1980
Snowmass, Colorado
Neil Morgan
Skidmore, Owings & Merrill,
Richard Keating, Design Partner
Wood frame
Redwood siding, metal-clad wood windows

This residence is located alongside a ski run in Snowmass, Colorado. The primary intent of the design is to respond to the unique ski-in/ski-out site, the views, and the surrounding aspen groves. To preserve as many trees as possible, the house is oriented perpendicular to the slope of the hill. The building steps down in the direction of the primary views, conforming to height restrictions and providing outdoor decks at the tree-top level with sightlines to the ski run and the mountains beyond. The building orientation and the use of glass are carefully arranged to provide maximum solar heat gain in winter and balanced views, predominantly to the north. Special attention has been paid to the entertainment function of the house and the dramatic master bedroom and bath.

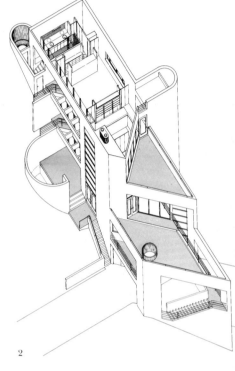

1   Site plan
2   Axonometric
3   Woodrun Street frontage

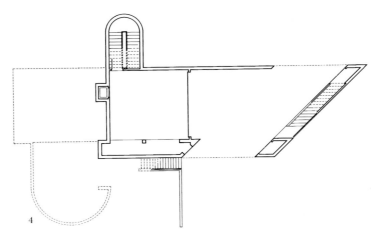

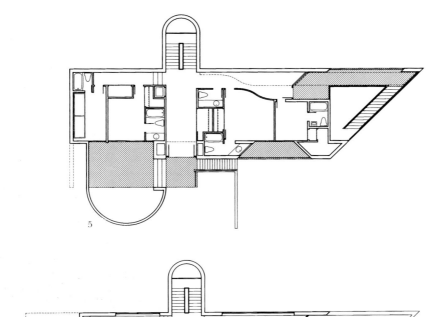

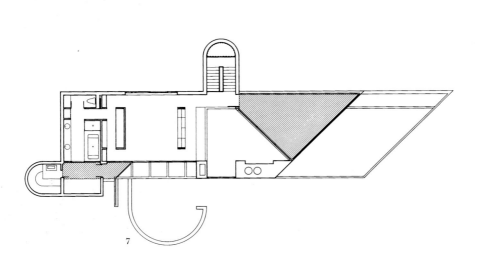

8

9

10

# 4949 Yoakum

Design/Completion 1980/1982
Houston, Texas
3,200 square feet
Skidmore, Owings & Merrill,
Richard Keating, Design Partner
Wood frame
Stucco

Built on a 60 x 125 foot lot in an urban
area of Houston, this house provides the
anonymity and security desired by the
owner as well as openness to the garden
and sunlight. Hidden behind a vine-
covered wall, the house is entered through
a garden court. All major trees on the site
were preserved and full advantage was
taken of a monolithic windowless party
wall along the southern property line.
Internal functions accommodate a
bedroom and upper level deck as well as
a galley kitchen serving a large
entertainment and dining area. The
exterior expression of the house is left to
the patterns of windows cut into ivy-
covered walls (a strong tradition in the
neighborhood); the focus is on the quality
of living within, and the experience of
sunlight and landscape without sacrificing
security or privacy.

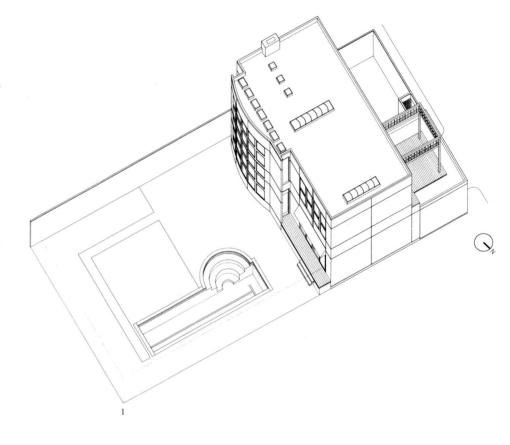

1

2

3

3   Master bedroom
4   Living room
5   Garden wall of living room

4

# Santa Monica Beach Hotel

Design 1987
Santa Monica, California
Michael McCarty
250,000 square feet (160 rooms)
Skidmore, Owings & Merrill,
Richard Keating, Design Partner

The Santa Monica Beach Hotel was to have been located on one of the most beautiful beaches in California. The site encompasses the former estate of 1930s film star Marion Davies, which was destroyed by fire leaving only an historic guest house.

The hotel is low-rise and scaled to minimise impact on the beachfront. The mass of the building is broken up around three courtyards, in keeping with the character of neighboring homes. The architecture is kept simple in order to create an elegant backdrop for the special landscaping program and the extensive collection of sculpture, paintings, and other pieces by Los Angeles artists.

Rooms are oriented around two of the courtyards which face the beach. The third courtyard faces the coastal access road and provides a gracious and distinct streetfront and entry.

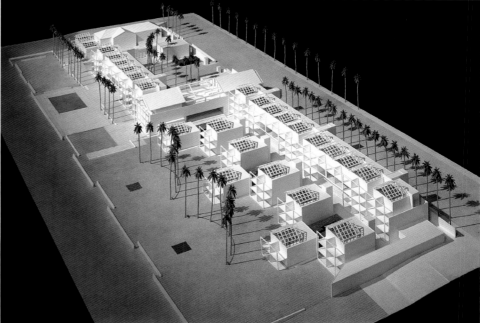

1

2

1  Beach view
2  Model: view from the south
3  View from Palisades Park
4  View from rooms toward bungalows
5  Ocean frontage

3

4

5

# Katsu-ura Condominiums

Design 1988
Katsu-ura, Japan
Taisei Corporation
380,000 square feet (425 units)
Skidmore, Owings & Merrill,
Richard Keating, Design Partner

Sited on a bluff on the Bossa Peninsula in Japan, the Katsu-ura Condominiums present a dramatic silhouette against the sky and provide residents with far-reaching and unobstructed views of the Pacific Ocean to the southeast and southwest. The siting of the 425 units allows for southern sun exposure for every unit and for common outdoor space.

The design of the complex was conceived to complement the rugged topography and fragmented geology of the area. Two 18-story, single-corridor slabs are juxtaposed on the site. Conceptually, the project was planned as one long structure disjoined into two pieces and connected at the top by a four-story bridge.

The bridge creates a grand portal 14 stories high and 157 feet wide. Approaching the project on a meandering road from the nearby fishing village of Katsu-ura, the portal is seen above, symbolically celebrating the point where the earth meets the sky. Entry into the development is through a long tunnel, creating a dramatic arrival at the portal and large circular motor court.

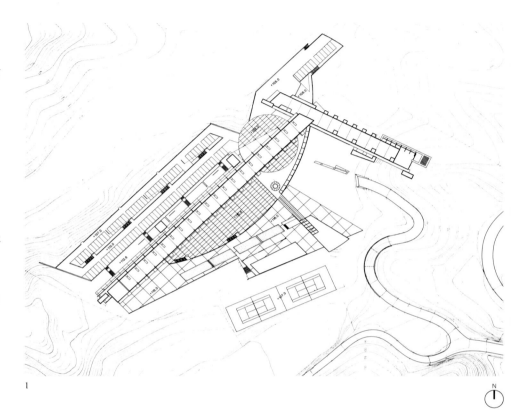

1

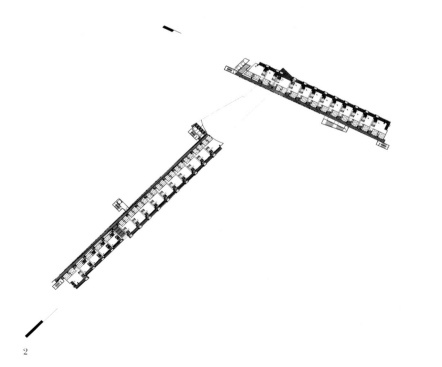

2

204

3

4

5

6

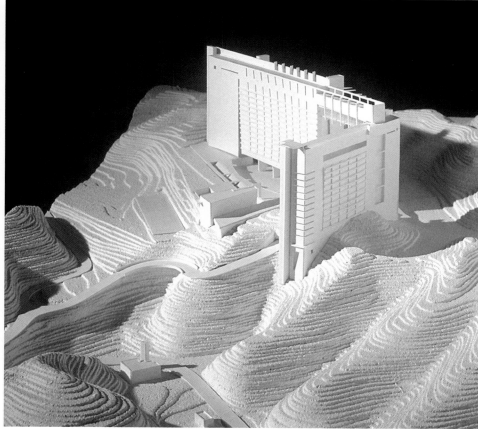

7

# Ocean Boulevard Condominiums

Design 1989
Long Beach, California
The Mendik Company
550 units
Skidmore, Owings & Merrill,
Richard Keating, Design Partner
Precast concrete, glass

The project was designed in two phases to attract the growing number of people moving to the area of Long Beach, California. One 30-story tower and one 45-story tower are placed on the ends of the site and angled to minimize obstruction of ocean views from buildings to the north of the development. The north sides of the towers are parallel with the existing urban grid in order to integrate the project with the rest of downtown. The south sides face the ocean with unimpeded views of the nearby harbor and beach, and Catalina Island in the distance.

The 550 units were all designed with balconies, large, tinted-glass windows, and elegant interior spaces. Some are two stories, and corner units have a 270 degree view of the coast and city.

At the top of each tower is a helipad cantilevered off one extreme, giving the buildings a dramatic skyline presence.

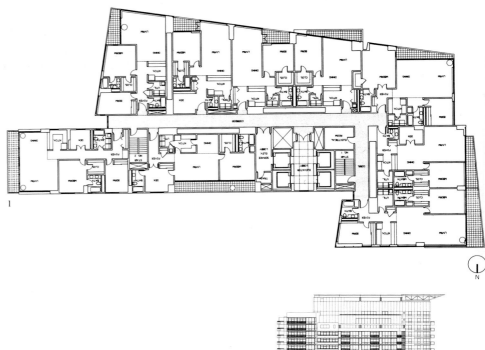

1

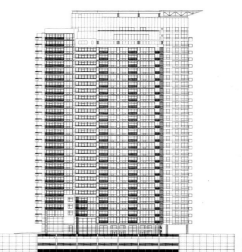

1   Site plan
2   South facade
3   First and second phase

2

3

4    4–5   Facade
5      6   Base
6      7   Entry
7      8   Waterfront view

## Montecito Residence

Design 1994
Montecito, California
4,000 square feet

Organized on a 3.5-acre site with a
pre-existing guest house, this design
establishes a clarity of back and front,
entry and circulation, privacy and view.
From the entry motor court with guest
parking, the sequence of movement flows
past a courtyard and vineyard to the front
door. The private garage functions from
the same courtyard but, with blind doors
and internal access to the house, does not
detract from the more formal sequence of
arrival.

The house is linear in plan with a clear
architectural bias toward the internal
property, the vineyard, the garden, and
ultimately the view to the Channel Islands.
All this is planned to accommodate the
indoor/outdoor lifestyle made possible by
the warm climate; the dominant "room"
becomes a two-story semi-screened deck
with a commanding view and an edge of
water created by the flush lap pool and
hot tub.

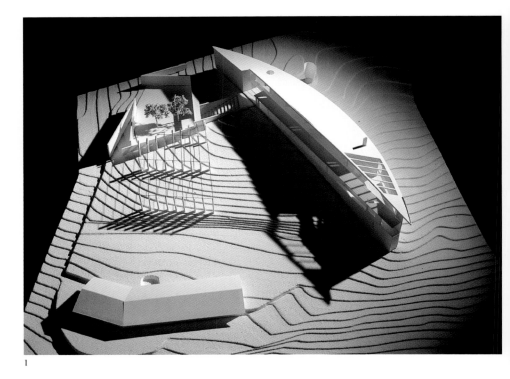

1

1 Model: view from the south
2 Main level
3 Second level

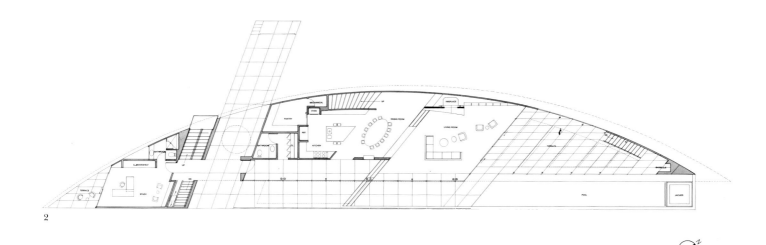

2

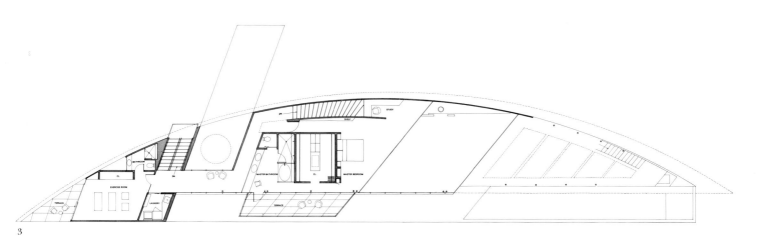

3

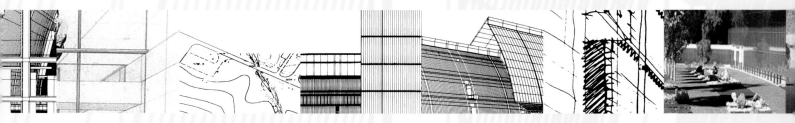

The evolution of a group of individuals brought together initially by my definition of what the culture of SOM meant to me, and ultimately by the merger with DMJM to form DMJM Keating, is in my mind a natural and logical extension of service and potential. While office buildings have been the hallmark of our work, the reality has been the solving of large, complex physical problems within urban and economic parameters that could and should be adapted to a larger and perhaps more fundamental set of our society's needs. DMJM provides the ideal basis from which to deal with urban infrastructure, military, governmental, and public sector work. The merger of our group with DMJM reflects the changes occurring in our society, and the demands that our foreign clientele is making on American technology.

While this new work ranges from urban rail interventions (such as the Alameda Corridor) to airports, hospitals, prisons, and bridges, perhaps the most compelling and telling is a scheme for the Laser Interferometer Gravitational Organization (LIGO). In a pair of laboratories at extreme ends of rural USA, theoretical gravitational waves traveling through the universe may be detected striking the surface of the earth and interrupting a pair of 2.5-mile-long lasers. A scheme was sought that would transform this otherwise simple lab/tech accommodation into a facility that visually celebrated the sheer length of the laser labs (not unlike the linear accelerator at Stanford). Since these laboratories are perennially in funding crisis, and visiting dignitaries are welcome for this reason, we added a ring of parking so that the purpose of the lab could be readily perceived from the beginning of a visit, and the architectural clarity of the purpose could be evocative of Myron Goldsmith's solar telescope on Kitt Peak near Tucson, Arizona.

The correction facilities that have become a major source of work are interesting examples of site planning in that they are often placed in what some might perceive as unimportant landscape. In California, this translates into the desert or the back end of cities.

I think this can be different without spending any more money; Harry Weese's jail in Chicago is a good example. We hope in the near future to work on the relationship to a desert environment. Moreover, without spending increases and without entering into the politics of complacency about anti-social behaviours, isn't there a ripe opportunity to clarify the transitions from freedom to incarceration? What about the potential for expressing and exalting the best of mankind as a counterpoint to the lowliness of incarceration. Would a "room of enlightenment" along the forced passages to meals or exercise become a means to touch at least one prisoner's thoughts? Aren't there architectural means to create positive messages, or at least a potential that has yet to be explored? It is our goal to engage this problem.

It seems that a fresh approach can benefit each of the DMJM-type projects and our work can touch the less elitist aspects of the built environment in positive ways. Having already honed our design attitudes to meet the aggressive economic positions of some of America's top developers (Hines, Crow, Lincoln, and Maguire Thomas), it is proving to be a recurring need for us to bring that skill and experience directly to private corporations and government entities.

Similarly, perhaps the most potent new direction that may yet emerge for DMJM Keating is an ability to serve our leading politicians, especially at the city and county levels, with infrastructure know-how and design vision. Our cities are in dire economic condition, yet the potential of evolving a synergy by thinking strategically and planning airports, or convention centers, or transit, or open space amenities, is available and would sustain a larger vision than that which is simply political or economic. Planning departments are often without the power or the skills to set this type of thinking in motion. It should become the purview of architectural leadership in the Dan Burnham tradition that brings a collaboration together in service to those in power. This is the inherent goal of DMJM Keating.

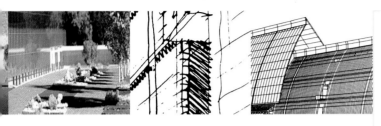

## New Directions

# Laser Interferometer Gravitational Observatory (LIGO)

Design 1994
Livingston, Louisiana and Hanford, Washington
Caltech/MIT
560 acres
Steel structure
Metal panels, concrete

Together, the LIGO and NIF projects represent the unique collaboration of architecture and engineering that in many ways was the impetus for the formation of DMJM Keating. In both cases, the importance of accommodating research and technology was far greater than the structure itself. However, it is our contention that architecture can support the purposes of such facilities, in terms of both quality and function. Both programs involved accommodating sophisticated scientific equipment and support spaces.

In the case of LIGO, the equipment (in very basic terms) measured the effect of gravity on light. The measurements advance, and are ultimately hoped to confirm, various theories about the universe and its formation.

In both projects, the enclosure was designed to allow for a greater emphasis on the special needs of the interior. LIGO was designed to enhance the simple beauty of the form created by the main station and its 13,123-foot-long laser arms that extend to form a right-angle. The focus was on the landscaped berm that would allow for visitor observation from above and aid in the conceptual understanding (and therefore funding) of the effort without significant interference or breach of security.

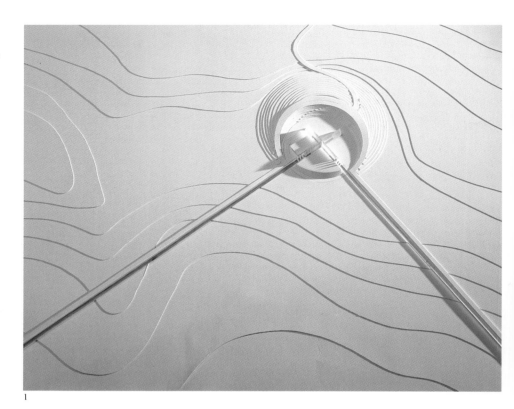

1

1   Site plan

# National Ignition Facility (NIF)

Design 1995
Livermore, California
Lawrence Livermore Laboratory
200,000 square feet
Steel structure
Metal panels, concrete

The NIF project accommodates lasers running along both sides of the building, in mirrored corridors that focus on a single point.

The mirrors amplify the energy of the lasers to create energy equivalent to that of the Sun. Ultimately, the purpose of the experiment was to derive self-generating energy from fusion.

The design concept was based on creating a center for the support facilities. The building was surrounded by a pool of water that would serve as a cooling pond for the facility, which has critical temperature requirements. The structure was taken to the exterior of the building to provide an uninterrupted interior space.

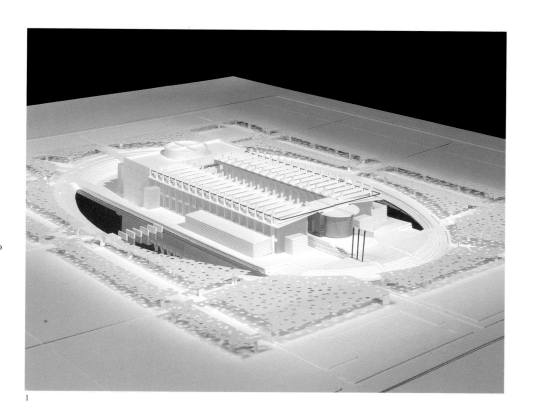

1

1   View of model

# SA Land Master Plan

Design 1995
Bangkok, Thailand
SA Land
12,000,000 square feet

The development of this master plan will play a critical role in Bangkok's growth as the city moves quickly into the 21st century. The project's functional priority is to accommodate 800,000 transit passengers a day (800 buses an hour) in the combined bus/rail terminal. Other components include retail, office, hotel, and parking.

While the project seeks to integrate itself within the context of the city, it remains a visible point of difference. The towers and main retail component form a strong street facade, accented by the entries which will feature graphics and electronic media devices. These elements combine to create an active retail frontage to tie into the existing street wall of Phahonyothin Road. Pushing the vehicular entries to the perimeter of this street facade allows for uninterrupted pedestrian circulation for the entire length of the project. This critical mass of retail frontage will have the ability to stimulate additional development.

*Continued*

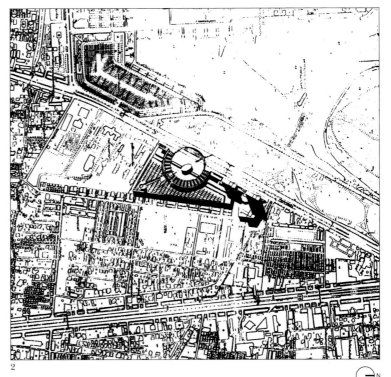

1

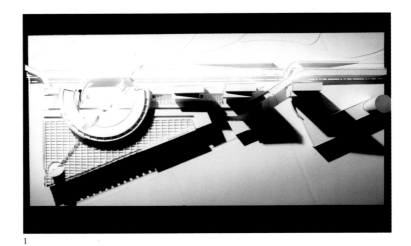

2

1 Model
2 Site plan
3 Transit station and retail center

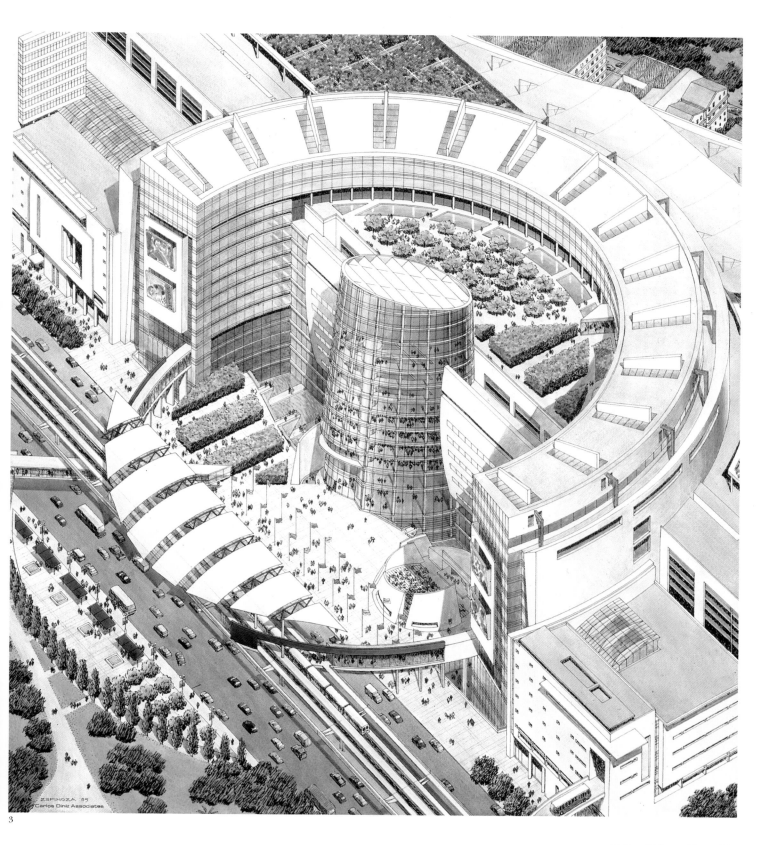

3

While pedestrian circulation is continuous, the strong street wall is interrupted by the creation of a grand plaza which forms the portal into the terminal and extends the project's character beyond the boundaries of its site. The plaza serves as a focal point for outdoor public activity, and also provides the city with space to breath. This break in the density of the city creates a space strong enough to act as the threshold to the terminal and large enough to handle the sheer number of commuters that will pass through it.

The elevated train station and park-side bus drop-off are also linked to this space by their positioning and architecture, which relates to the implied circle of the plaza. The plaza's landscaping, pools, and fountains are brought into the interior of the project, blurring the line between public and private space.

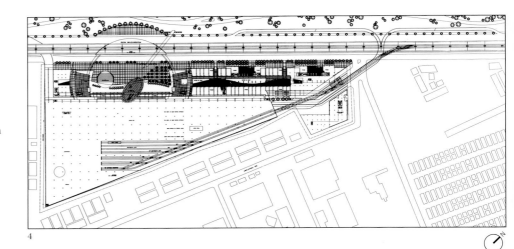

4

4   Level 1 plan
5   Retail center

5

# National Museum of Korea

Competition 1995
Seoul, South Korea
Associate architect: Hee-Lim Architects
1,000,000 square feet
Reinforced concrete
Cast-in-place concrete, granite, wood, dichroic glass, stainless steel, ceramic tile

The program includes 1 million square feet accommodated in two wings—a main gallery wing and an education wing—housing curatorial and educational functions, children's museum and special areas. The site plan was based on 'secularizing' the museum from the pervasive urbanity which surrounds it. Historic precedent was found in the legacy of important Korean buildings, many of which are walled environments. A perimeter wall serves to organize the museum and garden, and is penetrated by portals which are symbolic of the transition from present to past and future, and of a country in transition.

The underlying concept of the building and its grounds is a recurring balancing of positive and negative; open and closed; history and future; summer and winter; urban and pastoral.

*Continued*

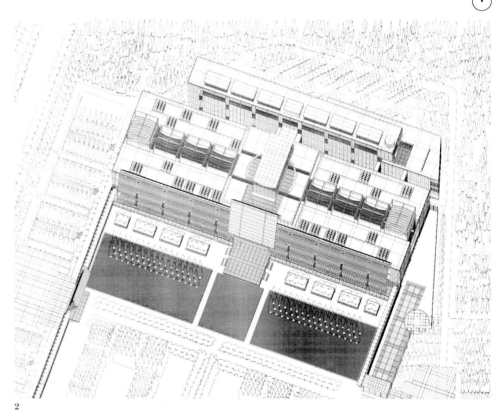

1

N

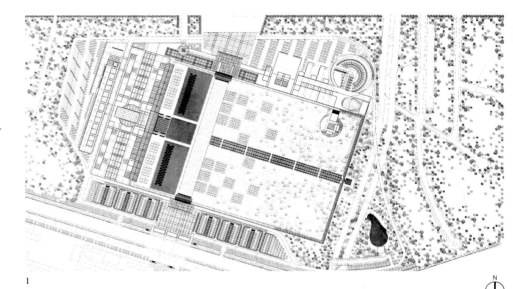

2

1 Site plan
2 Building axonometric
3 Section through entry promenade
4 Elevation

3

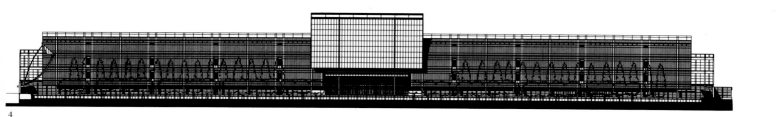

4

The site is exceptional in its auspicious geographic relationship to the city of Seoul. The simple diagram of the design belies the powerful effect of the garden that is invoked by long avenues of trees reflected in huge pools of water. While on one hand the facade of the museum is an aspect of containment, or wall of the national garden, it is also a representation in color, form, and materials of a wide range of Korean artifacts, from pottery to palatial roof-lines. The galleries themselves accommodate exhibits ranging from hand-held objects to stupas and pagodas up to 10 stories in height.

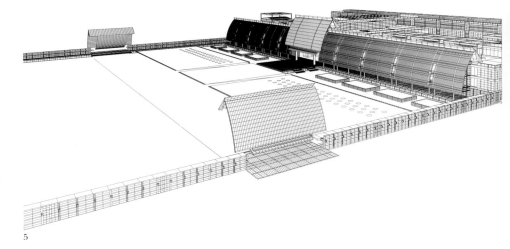

5

6

5   Building perspective
6   Site section: building and garden
7   Derivative of gateway
8   Building section
9   Garden walkway and museum facade

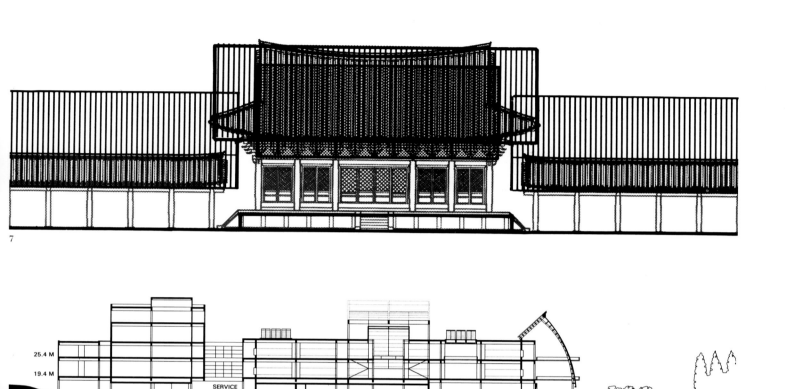

7

8

9

# Samsung Aerospace Advanced Park

Design 1995
Sachon, South Korea
Samsung Corporation
Associate architect: Samwoo Architects
8,000,000 square feet (site area: 618 acres)

The goal of this master plan is to develop a comprehensive facility plan for an aerospace industrial complex that focuses on state-of-the-art commercial aircraft manufacturing and assembly as well as other aviation-related facilities such as testing, maintenance, component production, and warehousing. The master plan also includes an administrative/ research and welfare complex that supports the workforce with commercial, recreational, educational, research, cultural, and health facilities. The master planning study includes a new utility infrastructure development and airfield requirements.

Functionally, the design of each of the buildings within the master plan is predicated on a rectangular plan based on standard building module dimensions. As the most flexible and economical configuration for the required program, the rectangular plan is altered only when dictated by a special purpose. Given the nature of aircraft assembly lines, storage systems, and office systems (furniture, lighting, etc.), these buildings, organized on an orthogonal system, maximize the usage of each square foot of space.

1

2

3

4

5

## Tokyo Electron America Inc.

Design/Completion 1995/1997
Austin, Texas
Taisei America Corporation
100,000 square feet (site area; 59 acres)

This project involves the master planning and design of four phases of buildings outside of Austin, Texas for a company that manufactures the machinery for computer chip fabrication. The master plan arranges the buildings around the hilltop site and, through landscaping, the hill is reinforced as a place and focal point for the project.

The two office buildings are oriented to maximize views toward downtown Austin as well as to form an entrance to the project. The buildings rely on a language of seamless, large-scale moves in an attempt to magnify the tension between foreground and background; an expression of our contemporary condition in which the seemingly infinite scale of the universe can be held within something the size of a computer chip.

The office building is seen as a "processor" of sales and service, its mirrored glass envelope a slice of silicon slipped between an overhanging roof and a base of rough-cut stone. The parts and training building is seen as a "stronghold box" of company information. The building's slotted windows provide strategic views to the outside while its concrete shell protects the techniques and parts necessary to prolong the products' lives.

The lobby—a two-story space running through the office building—is the "gate", connecting views down to Austin with the axis up to the hilltop. The various polished and mirrored surfaces in the lobby begin to blur boundaries and expand space—a metaphor for the dematerialization of matter by information.

1

2

1    Motor court
2    Lobby
3–4  Site plan

228

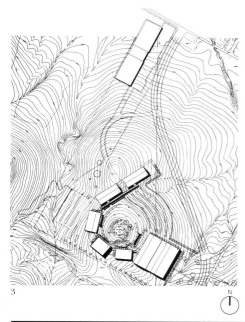

3

4

# Korea Development Bank

Design/Completion 1995/1999
Seoul, South Korea
The Korea Development Bank
Associate architect: Hee-Rim Architects
1,000,000 square feet
Steel
Glass, aluminum

The new headquarters building for the Korea Development Bank occupies a prominent site on Seoul's Jeoudo Square. The site has a unique civic position as it is within close proximity of the National Assembly building and the Han River (a strong cultural element in Seoul), and borders a significant open space reminiscent of Tiananmen Square in Beijing or Central Park in New York.

The bank is the financial engine for the substantial transition currently underway in Korea which will shape the country's emergent role in the 21st century. Philosophically, the premise of the design concept is to express a sense of stability and permanence appropriate for the bank, as well as a progressive spirit representative of the bank's role in the growth of the Korean economy.

Architecturally, the headquarters building has the responsibility of both containing and continuing the adjacent open space and acknowledging the National Assembly which anchors the adjacent boulevard. By placing the banking hall at the corner, its unique shape creates the deflection toward the government building; at the same time the cornice line nine stories above continues the edge of the open space.

*Continued*

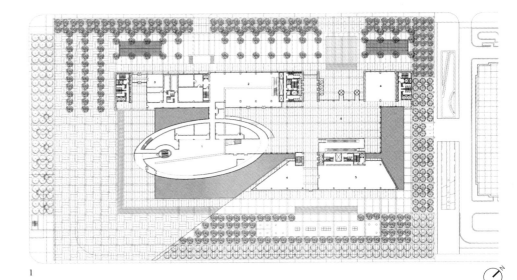

1

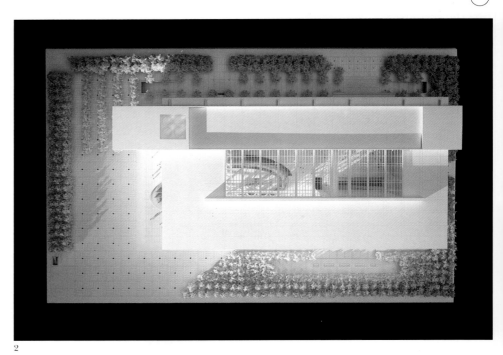

2

1   Site plan
2   Building plan
3   View through atrium

3

Beyond the banking hall are two wings of an office building separated by a grand internal atrium. Each wing derives its external character from the adjacent and varying urban condition. The east wing faces the open space, so maintains a grand scale. It appears to float above the trees and derives its geometry from a wide angle of vision in the foreground. Into this mass is carved a very large window that punctuates the facade at a scale that serves as a focus.

The banking hall is the focus of the building and serves allegorically as the rock in the river of transition that represents stability and permanence.

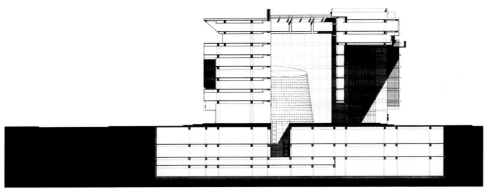

4

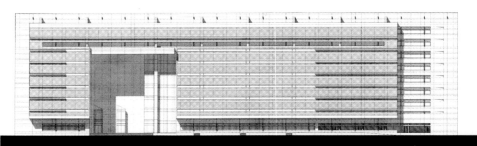

5

6

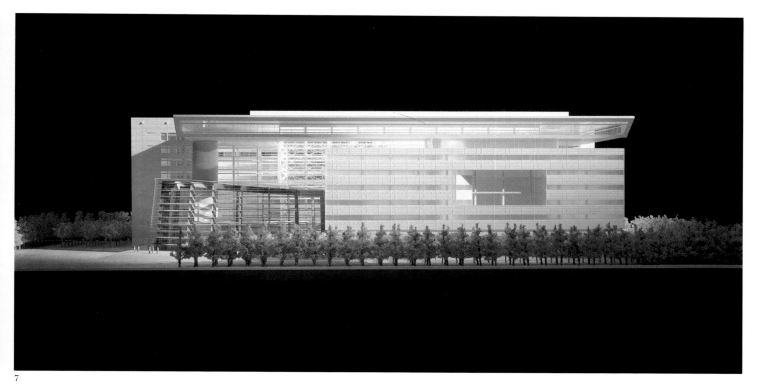

7

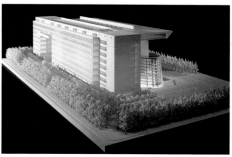

8

4  Section north–south
5  Northwest elevation
6  Southwest elevation
7  Southeast elevation
8  West view
9  East view

9

## Firm Profile

# The Process and the People

The complexity of this scale of architecture involves a multitude of decisions and a diverse group of people and talents. For the past 20 years, a relatively cohesive team of individuals has contributed greatly to the success of our work. Over that period, my role has expanded from design to include establishing the setting and process for design, and orchestrating and encouraging design by others. Beyond design, a set of values about making buildings from a technical point of view—details, materials, documentation—has been a significant legacy from the Chicago experience and SOM. Collaboration with other disciplines— engineering, landscape, lighting— as well as with contractors and subcontractors, has played an extensive role in this work.

Along the way, I have sought the finest of colleagues and have found a new pleasure in architecture that comes from their success, recognition, and growth. In design, Paul Danna and Jose Palacios have emerged as significant architects whose efforts and qualities have allowed me to work over a broader scope of the design process than would otherwise have been possible. Their skills have also allowed the sustenance of a dialogue from concept to detail in which my own level of involvement can vary according to time available and project demand without compromising decision-making. Cory Ticktin and Li Wen are assuming similar responsibilities as important members of the core design team.

The design process includes management, and management includes design, which is to say that each client relationship is fundamental to the resultant quality and success of the design. Ensuring this aspect of architecture has been the role of Michael Mann and Bob Newsom who have enjoyed full careers as architects, creating quality through their skill in drawing the best from clients and staff.

The work is fully dependent on the quality of the interpretation to the contractors and subcontractors as well as the strategic decisions along the way that affect the constructability and affordability. In this regard, Rob Jernigan is exceptional. Through wisdom and persuasion, the builders gain a sense of ownership in the design and quality of its outcome.

For 20 years I have sustained and nurtured a practice in interior design that has given me great personal satisfaction as well as a means to extend my interest in finishes, detail and materials to this more personal scale of architecture. At the same time it has also provided an opportunity to work more directly for the individuals within the office buildings which, until recently, have provided so much of our work. Beginning with a collaboration at SOM and subsequently KMJR, Lauren Rottet has become one of the leading interior designers practicing in the U.S. today with numerous projects to her credit. Her work has focused on high end corporate interiors as well as strategic programming and space planning.

# The Process

The process has grown into an understandable format of dealing with the thousands of decisions by organizing them, as much as possible, along a timeline from the general to the specific and similarly recognizing that all decisions are either objective or subjective. In proceeding from general to specific decisions, we are able to bring our clients along the decision path in a manner that doesn't upset the timeliness of activity. The objective decisions are each optimized. These are the decisions that are absolutely necessary to the building, including all the engineering (minimum structure; least cost building systems) and the matters of building efficiency. The subjective decisions of color, scale, material, and texture can then be made in the context of what remains between the necessary and the budget. Once this process, is adopted as part of the design process and specifically by the designer, the expenditures are prioritized appropriately, assuming the budget is adequate to begin with.

Finally, language—the means of reducing the essence of the building expression to the mind's eye through words—is our means of focusing design decisions towards a common set of values. The essentials of reverence and balance drove much of the design of the Ecology building. For the Rangers Stadium, knowing that the excessive parking lots were both the real problem as well as the opportunity set that design in motion. The redesign/ renovation projects each involve a search for the "genetic code" of the existing building and require reprogramming rather than designing a transplant. Our work on the Memphis Brooks Museum started with the James Gamble Rogers classic and reinterpreted its proportions and symmetrical organization in the new addition. The Katsu-ura condominiums incorporated the poetic imagery of Sverre Fehn in the building at the top of a hill.

# Biographies

Richard Keating began his career at Skidmore Owings & Merrill in 1968 where he was a designer on numerous international projects, new towns, large office buildings, research facilities and retail centers. In 1976, he was asked to open an office for SOM in Houston, Texas which he built to a practice of 200 architects, engineers and interior designers. In ten years the office designed and built nearly 40 million square feet. It was during this time that Keating gained a national design reputation. The unforeseen economic downturn in Houston and Dallas in the latter part of the 80s prompted Keating's move to assume charge of SOM Los Angeles which coincided fortuitously with the emergence of greater architectural opportunities in the West Coast and Pacific Rim markets.

The projects completed during Keating's years at SOM include landmark highrise buildings such as the Allied Bank Plaza in Houston, Texas (now First Interstate Plaza); Trammell Crow Center, Dallas, Texas; Texas Commerce Tower, Dallas, Texas; Renaissance Center renovation, Dallas, Texas; and the Gas Company Tower, Los Angeles, California. This period also saw the establishment of an interior design practice within SOM and the direction of award-winning projects for banks, law firms, financial institutions and hotels. The success of the Houston and Los Angeles offices of SOM was largely due to the abilities and talent of an exceptional group of professionals. This nucleus of individuals has worked together for over 17 years, moving from Houston to Los Angeles and ultimately leaving SOM to evolve into DMJM Keating.

Keating earned his architectural degree from the University of California, Berkeley. He is frequently invited to speak on a range of topics affecting architecture and is currently the 1996 Howard Friedman Professor at the University of California, Berkeley.

Paul Danna graduated with distinction from both the University of Michigan and the Harvard Graduate School of Design. His education also included a year at the Institute of Architecture and Urban Design Studies in New York as a student in the advanced design workshop. While at Harvard, Danna was awarded the James Templeton Kelly Prize, one of Harvard's highest honors for architectural design. Mr Danna also received the Skidmore, Owings & Merrill Traveling Fellowship, an annually awarded, national prize for design excellence.

Danna joined Skidmore Owings & Merrill in 1986 and worked in both the Houston and Los Angeles offices where he became an associate of the firm. Prior to that, he worked with various nationally renowned firms, among them, I.M. Pei & Partners; Krueck and Olsen Architects and Machado-Silvetti Architects.

Danna was a partner and founding member of Keating Mann Jernigan Rottet, and he has directed the design of a large variety of project types including office buildings, mixed use developments, high technology facilities and corporate headquarters. His work has appeared in numerous publications and has been exhibited at galleries in New York, Chicago, Los Angeles, the Art Institute of Chicago and in traveling exhibits abroad.

*I first met Rick as a finalist for the Skidmore, Owings & Merrill Traveling Fellowship. He was among a dozen SOM partners who conducted the requisite interview. The qualities I observed that day, Rick's energy, keen wit and inquisitiveness led me to accept a position for SOM in Houston two years later upon graduation.*

*Over the past ten years as employee, partner and friend, we have had the opportunity to design more buildings than our respective years might suggest. These years have not only taken me to places around the world, but also from SOM in Houston and Los Angeles through the formation of our own firm, Keating Mann Jernigan Rottet, and now to DMJM Keating. Throughout all of this, Rick has continued to embody those qualities that I first observed and to demonstrate others that are equally valuable to me and the group of us who have worked together for so many years. He has created opportunities through his business sense, talent, imagination and ability to communicate. To me, he has been the model of an architect striving to regain for the profession the leadership and influence that I imagine figures such as Burnham once possessed.*

*I recently heard a discussion on the importance of mentorship in our profession. One speaker characterized the relationship as a progressive transference of information and inspiration for which there were three phases: the giving of responsibility, authority and credit. As I reflect on the time we have spent working together, it is clear to me that our relationship has been a classic example of the mentor–apprentice dynamic. Rick has exposed me to as much knowledge and opportunity as I could absorb, has given me the responsibility to act on those opportunities, the authority to guide them and the credit for their results. While our entire team possesses many strengths, the ability to give in this manner has become one of the most important aspects of our culture. In my mind, this continues to be paramount in our success.*

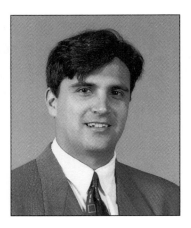

Jose Palacios graduated with honors from Texas A&M University. His interests varied from physics and mathematics to philosophy and architecture, spending nearly nine years in academia in various institutions in South America, Europe and the United States. The influence of this experience is evident in the geometry, composition and precision of detail that characterizes his work. He brings a unique level of enthusiasm and energy to design, eliciting a high level of creativity from design team members.

Palacios joined Skidmore, Owings & Merrill in 1986, working in both Houston and Los Angeles offices. He achieved the level of associate in 1988 and was the senior designer on a number of office and mixed-use projects. In 1990, Palacios left SOM to become a founding principal of Keating Mann Jernigan Rottet. Over the past nine years, he has contributed to and led the design effort for numerous constructed projects, experience which is invaluable in the design process. These projects include highrise renovations, corporate headquarters, and complex public sector projects.

*If I could synthesize my years collaborating with Rick, I would say that our practice has had an emphasis on process and craft. In that "process" depends on collaboration and negates preconception, each of our roles is important in the ultimate success of a project.*

*Many things can be said about how the design process works, however, one thing is evident given the complexity of today's architectural criteria and the impact on deriving meaningful solutions. This one overriding factor is the duality that lies between nature and reason, analysis and synthesis. It is here that an architect's artistic sensibilities—imagination, intuition and creativity—must be combined with the methodical and pragmatic abilities like those of an engineer or accountant. Things seen in an instant can prove to be as important as those developed or discovered throughout the duration of a project.*

*Each of our projects acknowledges precedent yet contains a fresh recognition of what is known and what has yet to be discovered. This is what generates excitement. The most difficult aspect of a project is identifying the problem, underscored by site, physical and cultural context, function, user, client, budget construction technology and a myriad of other issues.*

*This basic formula is solved using clarity, rigor and a profound awareness of the importance of detail. The aesthetic value in our buildings is rooted in techtonics and craft. Details are used in many ways, to ensure the geometrical integration of a plan, to express a material's inherent nature, or to exalt the dialogue between solid and void. Equally important is the integration of life safety systems and other practical requirements often considered as architectural nuisances or simply forgotten in the techtonic fabric of a building and therefore in its aesthetic. Details that rely on craft and precision with an absence of style become the soul of a building. The love and passion of the craftsman translate into lasting value and transcendence. Craft and technical integrity are of great concern given that most buildings ought to be experienced in the human and physical context, not as willful expressions of journalistic documentation. At the end of the process, the goal is attained if a building serves its purpose well and transcends its time in a dignified manner.*

Robert Newsom, AIA, is a Senior Vice President of DMJM. Since joining the firm in 1993, he has led an effort to establish the firm as a leading architectural practice. Prior to joining DMJM, Newsom was president of Dworsky Associates, a Los Angeles architectural firm, where he directed project teams in the successful completion of numerous large scale projects. He was principally responsible for establishing the firm's reputation for outstanding client service, particularly in the public sector.

Newsom earned his Bachelor of Architecture degree from the University of Arizona in 1970. He has been the project director for more than 40 projects during his career, many prominent and award winning.

Michael Mann, AIA, graduated from the University of Oklahoma with a Bachelor of Science degree in Environmental design as well as a Master of Architecture degree. He brings a great deal of architectural and professional experience to his role in management. After joining Skidmore, Owings & Merrill in 1977, he was soon the project architect and senior designer on a number of projects including the 71 story Allied Bank Plaza. Mann was an Associate Partner and responsible for the administration and management of SOM, Los Angeles prior to leaving to establish Keating Mann Jernigan Rottet in 1990. Currently, Mann is a Vice President of DMJM and responsible for the fiscal management of DMJM Keating and its more complex projects.

Robert Jernigan, AIA, has applied his technical expertise to over 10 million square feet of complex architectural and interiors projects. He has achieved a unique level of respect for his ability to integrate an excitement for and understanding of design in construction. Much of the quality of the firm's work and execution of complex detail can be attributed to Jernigan's participation.

Jernigan was an Associate Partner of Skidmore, Owings & Merrill, having joined the firm in 1980. He left SOM in 1990 to establish Keating Mann Jernigan Rottet and is presently a Vice President of DMJM, directing the technical team of DMJM Keating. He has been and continues to be integral to the design of every project, applying his technical knowledge in early phases of design strategy and direction.

# Chronological List of Buildings & Projects
**(By year of project commencement)**

*Indicates work featured in this book
*(see Selected and Current Works).*

## Skidmore, Owings & Merrill
## Richard Keating, Design Partner

### 1980

First Federal Savings and Loan

**\*First Federal Savings and Loan**
  Little Rock, Arkansas
  158,000 square feet
  Completed: 1980

### 1982

Allied Bank Plaza

Tenneco Employee Center

Morgan Residence

4949 Yoakum Residence

**\*Allied Bank Plaza**
  Houston, Texas
  1,800,000 square feet
  Completed: 1982

**\*Tenneco Employee Center**
  Houston, Texas
  100,000 square feet
  Completed: 1982
  Design Partner: Richard Keating
  Architect: Skidmore, Owings & Merrill

**\*Morgan Residence**
  Snowmass
  Snowmass, Colorado
  4,000 square feet
  Completed: 1982
  Design Partner: Richard Keating
  Architect: Skidmore, Owings & Merrill

**\*4949 Yoakum**
  Houston, Texas
  3,200 square feet
  Completed: 1982
  Design Partner: Richard Keating
  Architect: Skidmore, Owings & Merrill

### 1983

Bank of the Southwest Competition

**\*Bank of the Southwest Competition**
  Houston, Texas
  2,300,000 square feet
  Design: 1983
  Design Partner: Richard Keating
  Architect: Skidmore, Owings & Merrill

## 1984

San Felipe Plaza

## 1985

Trammell Crow Center

## 1987

Texas Commerce Tower

Sun Bank Center

Santa Monica Beach Hotel

Pacific Atlas

Wilshire at Cañon

Wilshire at Robertson

**\*San Felipe Plaza**
Houston, Texas
1,000,000 square feet
Completed: 1984
Design Partner: Richard Keating
Architect: Skidmore, Owings & Merrill

**\*Trammell Crow Center**
Dallas, Texas
1,750,000 square feet
Completed: 1985
Design Partner: Richard Keating
Architect: Skidmore, Owings & Merrill

**\*Texas Commerce Tower**
Dallas, Texas
1,400,000 square feet
Completed: 1987
Design Partner: Richard Keating
Architect: Skidmore, Owings & Merrill

**\*Sun Bank Center**
Orlando, Florida
850,000 square feet
Completed: 1987
Design Partner: Richard Keating
Architect: Skidmore, Owings & Merrill

**\*Santa Monica Beach Hotel**
Santa Monica, California
250,000 square feet
Design: 1987
Design Partner: Richard Keating
Architect: Skidmore, Owings & Merrill

**\*Pacific Atlas**
Los Angeles, California
34-story tower, 45-story tower,
550-room hotel
Design: 1987
Design Partner: Richard Keating
Architect: Skidmore, Owings & Merrill

**\*Wilshire at Cañon**
Beverly Hills, California
75,000 square feet
Design: 1987
Design Partner: Richard Keating
Architect: Skidmore, Owings & Merrill

**\*Wilshire at Robertson**
Beverley Hills, California
75,000 square feet
Design: 1987
Design Partner: Richard Keating
Architect: Skidmore, Owings & Merrill

# 1988

**\*Wilshire at Elm**
Beverley Hills, California
54,000 square feet
Completed: 1988
Design Partner: Richard Keating
Architect: Skidmore, Owings & Merrill

**\*Stockley Park Competition**
London, England
250,000 square feet
Design: 1988
Design Partner: Richard Keating
Architect: Skidmore, Owings & Merrill

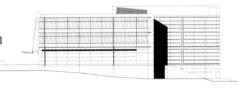

**\*3rd at Mission**
San Francisco, California
350,000 square feet
Design: 1988
Design Partner: Richard Keating
Architect: Skidmore, Owings & Merrill

**\*Aichi Corporate Headquarters**
Tokyo, Japan
64,000 square feet
Design: 1988
Design Partner: Richard Keating
Architect: Skidmore, Owings & Merrill

**\*Katsu-ura Condominiums**
Katsu-ura, Japan
380,000 square feet (425 units)
Design: 1988
Design Partner: Richard Keating
Architect: Skidmore, Owings & Merrill

**Singapore Master Plan**
Singapore
2,910,000 square feet (site area: 20 acres)
Design: 1988
Design Partner: Richard Keating
Architect: Skidmore, Owings & Merrill

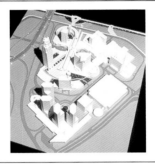

**Tower City Center**
Cleveland, Ohio
1,000,000 square feet
Design: 1988
Design Partner: Richard Keating
Architect: Skidmore, Owings & Merrill

**\*Wilshire Ambassador Competition**
Los Angeles, California
7,000,000 square feet
Design: 1988
Design Partner: Richard Keating
Architect: Skidmore, Owings & Merrill

## 1989

**\*Wilshire La Peer/ICM Headquarters**
Beverley Hills, California
82,000 square feet
Completed: 1989
Design Partner: Richard Keating
Architect: Skidmore, Owings & Merrill

**\*Renaissance Center**
Dallas, Texas
1,650,000 square feet
Completed: 1989
Design Partner: Richard Keating
Architect: Skidmore, Owings & Merrill

**\*Memphis Brooks Museum**
  Memphis, Tennessee
  80,000 square feet
  Completed: 1989
  Design Partner: Richard Keating
  Architect: Skidmore, Owings & Merrill

**\*Solana Marriott Hotel**
  Dallas, Texas
  185,000 square feet
  Completed: 1989
  Design Partner: Richard Keating
  Architect: Skidmore, Owings & Merrill

**\*Trammell Crow Center Irvine**
  Irvine, California
  Master plan: 1989
  Design Partner: Richard Keating
  Architect: Skidmore, Owings & Merrill

**\*Tokyo International Forum Competition**
  Tokyo, Japan
  1,400,000 square feet
  Design: 1989 (honorable mention)
  Design Partner: Richard Keating
  Architect: Skidmore, Owings & Merrill

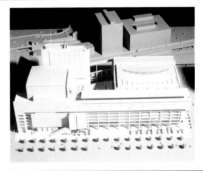

**\*Ocean Boulevard Condominiums**
  Long Beach, California
  550 units
  Design: 1989
  Design Partner: Richard Keating
  Architect: Skidmore, Owings & Merrill

# 1991

Gas Company Tower

American Honda Headquarters

**\*Gas Company Tower**
  Los Angeles, California
  1,750,000 square feet
  Completed: 1991
  Design Partner: Richard Keating
  Architect: Skidmore, Owings & Merrill

**\*American Honda Headquarters**
   Torrance, California
   800,000 square feet
   Completed: 1991
   Design Partner: Richard Keating
   Architect: Skidmore, Owings & Merrill

## Keating, Mann, Jernigan, Rottet
## 1990

Wilshire-Fairfax Office Building

Foremost Bank

**Wilshire-Fairfax Office Building**
   Los Angeles, California
   Design: 1990

**Foremost Bank**
   Kaohsiung, Taiwan
   Completed: 1990

## 1991

RTD Headquarters Competition

707 Wilshire Renovation

Texas Rangers Stadium

**\*RTD Headquarters Competition**
   Los Angeles, California
   600,000 square feet
   Design: 1991

**707 Wilshire Renovation**
   Los Angeles, California
   1,100,000 square feet
   Design: 1991

**\*Texas Rangers Stadium**
   Irving, Texas
   12,000 seats
   Design: 1991

## 1992

British Petroleum Plaza

## 1993

BMC Software Headquarters

Department of Ecology Headquarters

First National Bank San Diego

Opel-Kreisel Office Building

Santa Monica College Library Expansion

## 1994

Los Angeles International Airport
Master Plan

Los Angeles Convention Center
Transit Proposal

Montecito Residence

Laser Interferometer Gravitational
Observatory

Vietnam Airport

**\*British Petroleum Plaza**
Houston, Texas
480,000 square feet
Completed: 1992

**\*BMC Software Headquarters**
Houston, Texas
600,000 square feet
Completed: 1993

**\*Department of Ecology Headquarters**
Lacey, Washington
320,000 square feet
Completed: 1993

**\*First National Bank San Diego**
San Diego, California
580,000 square feet
Completed: 1993

**\*Opel-Kreisel Office Building**
Frankfurt, Germany
312,163 square feet
Design: 1993

**\*Santa Monica College Library Expansion**
Santa Monica, California
15,000 square feet
Design: 1993
Associate Architect: ROTOndi Architects

**\*Los Angeles International Airport
Master Plan**
Los Angeles, California
Master plan: 1994

**\*Los Angeles Convention Center
Transit Proposal**
  Los Angeles, California
  Planning study: 1994

**\*Montecito Residence**
  Montecito, California
  4,000 square feet
  Design: 1994

**\*Laser Interferometer Gravitational
Observatory (LIGO)**
  Louisiana and Washington
  Design proposal: 1994

**Vietnam Airport**
  Design proposal: 1994

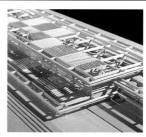

# 1994

10960 Wilshire Boulevard

**\*10960 Wilshire Boulevard**
  Los Angeles, California
  534,000 square feet
  Completed: 1994

# DMJM Keating
# 1995

SA Land Master Plan

Alameda Corridor Urban Design Proposal

National Museum of Korea

Hewlett Packard Business Center

Houston Industries Plaza

National Ignition Facility

Samsung Aerospace Advanced Park

**\*SA Land Master Plan**
  Bangkok, Thailand
  12,000,000 square feet
  Master plan: 1995

**Alameda Corridor Urban Design Proposal**
  Los Angeles, California
  20 miles
  Urban planning proposal: 1995

**\*National Museum of Korea**
Seoul, South Korea
1,000,000 square feet
Design: 1995
Associate architect: Hee-Lim Architects

**\*Hewlett Packard Business Center**
Atlanta, Georgia
600,000 square feet
Completed: 1995

**\*Houston Industries Plaza**
Houston, Texas
1,100,000 square feet renovation
Completed: 1995

**\*National Ignition Facility (NIF)**
Livermore, California
Design proposal: 1995

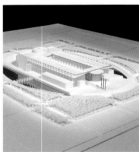

**\*Samsung Aerospace Advanced Park**
Sachon, Korea
2,500,000 square feet
Master plan: 1995

# 1996

International Center

**\*International Center**
Dallas, Texas
Phase 2: 215,000 square feet
Phase 3: 200,000 square feet
Completion: 1996

## 1997

San Bernardino Government Center

Tokyo Electron America Inc.

## 1998

Korea Development Bank

## 1999

Elihu M. Harris State Office Building

Galeria Jakarta

**\*San Bernardino Government Center**
San Bernardino, California
315,000 square feet
Completion: 1997

**\*Tokyo Electron America Inc.**
Austin, Texas
150,000 square feet
Completion: 1997

**\*Korea Development Bank**
Seoul, South Korea
1,000,000 square feet
Completion, 1998

**\*Elihu M. Harris State Office Building**
Oakland, California
700,000 square feet
Completion: 1999

**Galeria Jakarta**
Jakarta, Indonesia
775,000 square feet
Completion: 1999

# Bibliography

## Books

Arnell, Peter & Ted Bickford (eds). *Bank of the Southwest Competition*. New York: Rizzoli, 1983.

*Los Angeles Guide to Recent Architecture* Phillips, Dian. Artemis Publications, 1995, pp. 188, 190, 270.

*Gratte-ciel* (*Skyscrapers*). Norma Publications, Paris, 1995.

## National Press

"Skyscrapers." *National Geographic* (February 1989). (Keating/Texas Commerce Bank)

"The Sky's the Limit." *Newsweek* (November 1992).

## Architectural Press

*Architectural Record* (April 1994). (Opel-Kreisel Building)

*Architectural Record* (February 1995). (Houston Industries Plaza)

*Architectural Record* (lighting supplement, March 1995). (Houston Industries Headquarters)

*Architectural Record* (May 1992). (Gas Company Tower)

*Architectural Record* (October, 1994). (Department of Ecology Headquarters)

*Architecture* (April 1984). (Allied Bank Plaza)

*Architecture* (March 1990). (Memphis Brooks Museum)

*Architecture + Urbanism* (special feature, October 1990). (Richard Keating)

*Architecture*. (February 1988). (Texas Commerce Bank)

*Building Design & Construction* (cover story, November 1993). (British Petroleum Plaza)

"Enhancing the Public Image." *Architecture* (November 1992).

"Houston & Beyond." *Inland Architect* (March 1987). (Keating profile)

*Interiors* (February 1992). (Solana Marriott Hotel)

*l'Arca* (July 1994). (Washington State Department of Ecology)

"LTV Tower." *Progressive Architecture* (July 1985). (Trammell Crow Center)

"New State Office Buildings—Department of Ecology." *Cascadia Forum* (May 1994).

"Of the Land." *Architecture* (November 1990). (Solana Marriott Hotel)

"SOM at 50: The New Generation." *Interiors* (December 1986).

"SOM: A Legend in Transition." *Architecture* (February 1989).

*Texas Architect* (January 1994). (Solana Marriott Hotel)

*Texas Architect* (May 1995). (BMC Headquarters)

## Regional Press

*Atlanta Journal/Atlanta Constitution* (April 9, 1993). (Hewlett-Packard Center)

*Dallas Morning News* (August 10, 1991). (Texas Rangers Stadium)

*Dallas Morning News* (July 14, 1990). (Solana Marriott Hotel)

*Dallas Morning News* (June 1995). (International Center)

"Highrise Makeover." *Houston Chronicle* (December 2,1995). (Houston Industries Plaza)

"High Rise Profile: Richard Keating." *Dallas Morning News* (Business section, October 1990).

*Houston Business Journal* (May 4,1992).(British Petroleum Plaza)

*Houston Chronicle* (February 2, 1994). (Houston Industries Plaza)

*Houston Chronicle* (March 1, 1992). (British Petroleum Plaza, BMC Software Headquarters)

*Houston Chronicle* (November 8, 1992). (BMC Software Headquarters)

*Houston Post* (March 8, 1992). (British Petroleum Plaza)

*Oakland Tribune* (May 1995). (Elihu M. Harris State Office Building)

"Profile: Richard Keating." *Los Angeles Business Journal* (October 1994).

*San Diego Daily Transcript* (December 28,1993). (First National Bank San Diego)

*San Diego Union Tribune* (June 17,1990). (Keating profile, Houston's downtown)

*Seattle Daily Journal* (September 22, 1993). (Department of Ecology Headquarters)

# Acknowledgments

Architecture is only a game of the mind if the opportunities are not set in motion by others. Collaboration and a search for the best of ideas is the hallmark of our work. Our built projects not only reflect this principle, but simply could not exist without the numerous contributors to the opportunity at hand. From my parents that provided the education and stimulus, to the educators of special impact, I have been deeply blessed. Bill Browning in Salt Lake City and Spiro Kostof at Berkeley were early and potent mentors. Walter Netsch, Bruce Graham, Bill Hartman, Tom Eyerman, Chuck Bassett and Myron Goldsmith drew me to SOM and to a very great degree, sent me forth representing their interests. Netsch's unique passion and social conscience continued where Spiro left off, all of which was to serve me invaluably when Graham and Hartman sent me to boom-town Houston with an SOM franchise.

The talent drawn to that environment in that time sustained and gave extraordinary dimension to my efforts and ambitions. The pleasure of seeing today, nearly 20 years later, the continuity of those individuals mostly still working together and all in support of one another, is particularly gratifying. Michael Mann, Deanie Keating, Rob Jernigan, Deborah Lehman, Craig Hartman, Linda Richard, Bob Halvorson, Louis Skidmore, Mike Damore, Ray Kuca, Keith Boswell, Steve Zimmerman, Richard Riveire and Lauren Rottet created SOM Houston out of a set of common beliefs, largely self-defined and still serving today in each of our endeavors. At this point, the unique clients that brought the word "opportunity" to a new meaning for me could certainly start with Trammell and Harlan Crow at the Trammell Crow Company; Jeff Toia at Prudential; Hines Interests; Lincoln Property Company; and later in Los Angeles, Rob Maguire and Maguire Thomas Partners; Jerry Barag at Equitable Real Estate; David Barker and David George at Houston Industries; Max Watson at BMC Software, George Ross and Dennis Raney at Hewlett-Packard, and Dan Rosenfeld at the State of California. The move back to California brought two inseparable design partners to me and subsequently our work. Jose Palacios and Paul Danna began at SOM in Houston and were formative to the character we were able to forge in the more open vistas of California.

The "family" also expanded to include the special abilities and unique characteristics of Dan Allen, Dana Barbera, Chuck Crawford, Bruce Fullerton, Bill Gerstner, David Gonzalez, Liz Martin, Francine Mora, Stuart Morkun, Danette Riddle, Eric Smith, Joey Shimoda, Dana Taylor, Cory Ticktin, Li Wen, Todd Tuntland, Audrey Wu, David Wood, Kyle Yardley, Hormoz Ziaebrahimi, and most recently, Kim Day, Craig Fernandez, Jonathan Haynel, Bob Newsom, Ryan Smith and David Woo. So much of our group is the very definition of excellence with such strong personalities that it is fair to say that a larger bonding force than whatever I contribute is at work here. I can only attribute that to a common set of values in architecture, a pleasure in hard work, growing older and having fun at the same time.

The builders with whom we have a continuing relationship make each of our buildings, no matter what we have our heart set on. Warren Bellows in Houston and the extensive depth of his organization; Dinwiddie Construction has been the epitome of professionalism; Raymond Brochstein has provided quality millwork, teaching, counseling, professionalism and friendship; Flack + Kurtz and Joe Colaco of CBM Engineers have encouraged us with new opportunities, friendship and similar beliefs about architecture.

Our appreciation extends to the exceptional talent and commitment of Modelworks, Doug Jamieson, and Carlos Diniz who help us communicate our vision to others. Joe Aker and Nick Merrick have documented our work through photography for over 20 years, always capturing the essence of what we do.

Special acknowledgement is appropriate for Danette Riddle. To her I owe many debts, not the least of which is the quality and reality of this book.

## Photography Credits

Joe Aker: 22 (2); 26 (1); 27 (2); 32 (2); 33 (3); 41 (3); 46 (2); 50 (5–6); 51 (7); 52 (2); 53 (3); 54 (4-6); 55 (7); 56 (1); 65 (2); 67 (7); 74 (2); 75 (3); 88 (2); 89 (3); 90 (1); 91 (6–7); 92 (8); 94 (2); 95 (3); 96 (4); 97 (5–6); 98 (9-10); 100 (1–4); 101 (5); 110 (2); 111 (3); 118 (1); 119 (3); 120 (4–5); 121 (6); 122 (7); 123 (8); 124 (9); 125 (10); 126 (11); 127 (14); 135 (2); 136 (3–4); 137 (7–8); 139 (5); 140 (6–7) 141 (8); 142 (9–10); 143 (11–13); 146 (1–2); 147 (3); 148 (4); 149 (5–7); 151 (2); 152 (3–4); 153 (5–8); 175 (2); 177 (4); 199 (2); 200 (3–4); 201 (5); 202 (2); 205 (3); 206 (4–5); 207 (6–7); 209 (3); 211 (8); 216 (1); 217 (1); 226 (4); 227 (5)

Assassi: 159 (3)

R. Barnes: 46 (1); 49 (3); 50 (4)

Benny Chan: 218 (1)

Hedrich Blessing: 18 (1); 19 (2); 20 (3); 21 (4); 23 (3); 24 (4); 25 (5); 28 (1); 29 (3); 30 (4); 31 (5-6); 34 (4); 35 (5); 36 (6–7); 37 (8); 38 (9–11); 39 (12); 44 (8); 45 (9); 59 (2); 60 (3–5); 61 (6); 62 (7–9); 63 (10); 78 (5–6); 79 (8); 83 (2); 84 (5–6); 85 (7); 86 (8); 87 (9); 102 (2); 103 (3); 104 (4–6); 105 (7); 106 (8-9); 107 (10); 108 (11–12); 109 (13); 114 (1); 115 (2); 116 (4); 117 (5); 129 (3); 130 (4); 131 (5); 133 (7)

Wolfgang Hoyt: 40 (1); 42 (4-6); 43 (7)

R. Keating: 80 (1); 81 (3–5)

Mark Lohman: 57 (5); 64 (1)

Esto Photographics: 77 (3)

Strode-Eckert: 155 (2); 156 (3–4); 157 (5)

Adrian Velicescu: 230 (2); 231 (3); 232 (6); 233 (7–9)

# Index

Bold page numbers refer
to projects included in
Selected and Current Works.